# SACRED SINS

## DEVADASIS IN CONTEMPORARY INDIA

ARUN EZHUTHACHAN

TRANSLATED BY MEERA GOPINATH

hachette INDIA

First published in Malayalam in 2016 by D C Books
This translation first published in hardcover by Hachette India in 2023
(Registered name: Hachette Book Publishing India Pvt. Ltd)
An Hachette UK company
www.hachetteindia.com

This paperback edition published in 2025

SRD



Map on p. vii by Neelima P Aryan



ISBN 978-93-5731-388-9

Hachette Book Publishing India Pvt. Ltd
4th & 5th Floors, Corporate Centre,
Plot No. 94, Sector 44, Gurugram 122003, India

Typeset in Minion Pro 11.5/16.5
by R. Ajith Kumar, New Delhi

Printed and bound in India
by Manipal Technologies Limited, Manipal

MIX
Paper | Supporting responsible forestry
FSC™ C043100
www.fsc.org

# SACRED SINS

**Arun Ezhuthachan** is currently Trissur Chief Reporter at *Malayala Manorama*. His debut book, *Visudhapapangalude India* (*Sacred Sins*), received the Kerala Sahitya Akademi Award for the best travelogue in 2019. He has also received the media fellowship of National Foundation for India for his study on the social condition of devadasis.

**Meera Gopinath** teaches language and literature at an educational institute. She has worked with language in various roles – including anchoring, travel journalism, technical writing, content writing and teaching. Translation, with its inherent challenges, is something she enjoys, and she has translated books, stories and scripts. Meera lives in Bengaluru with her husband and children.

*To my parents,*
*who never set barriers to my journeys...*

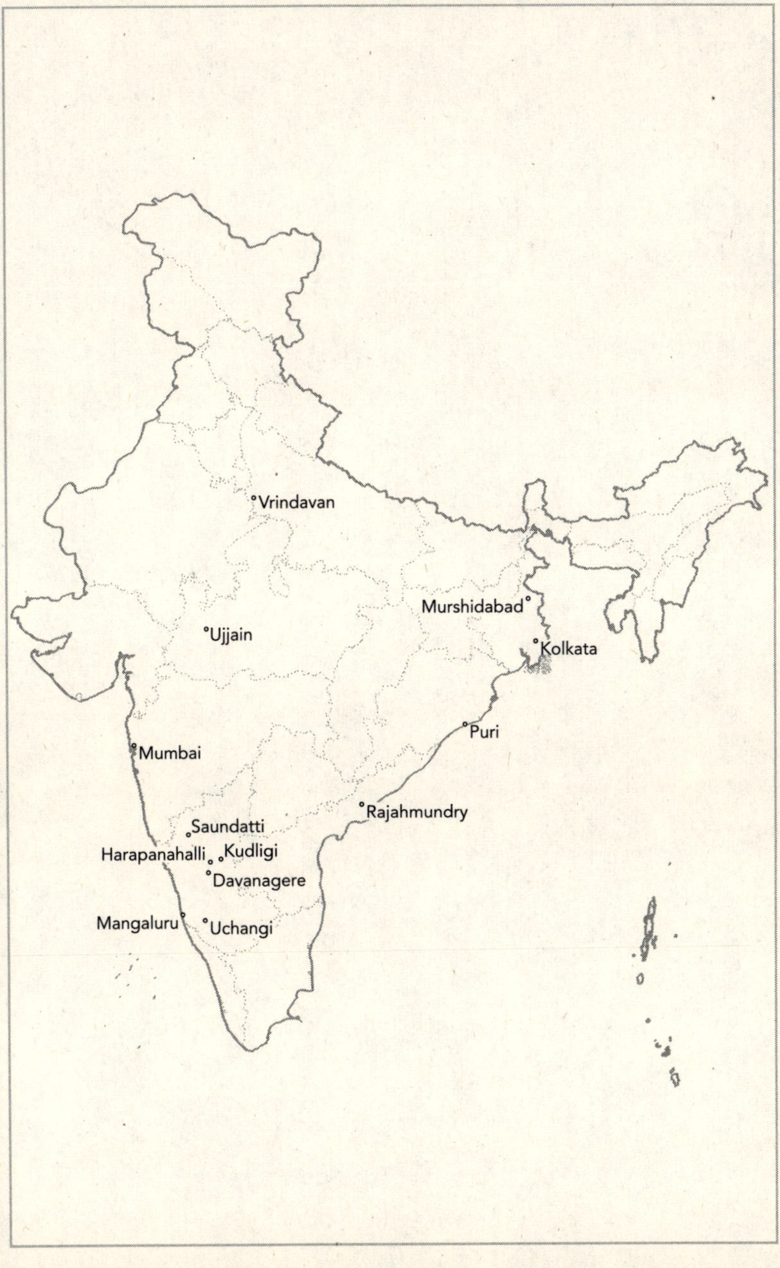
Vrindavan
Murshidabad
Ujjain
Kolkata
Puri
Mumbai
Rajahmundry
Saundatti
Harapanahalli
Kudligi
Davanagere
Mangaluru
Uchangi

# Contents

# Introduction

This is the English translation of my Malayalam book, *Visudhapapangalude India,* published in 2016. The travels recounted here began seven years prior to the first publication, in my journalist's search for a Sunday feature, and eventually led to the book which received the Kerala Sahitya Akademi Award in 2019.

What began as a short report on the closing of dance bars quickly turned into an extensive investigation spanning seven states and as many years. A conversation in Karnataka would lead me to Andhra Pradesh, a story heard in Mumbai would force me to go to Ujjain to learn more; in this manner I travelled extensively.

Everywhere I went, I saw how women were forced to bear the brunt of society's failings. Whether it was lower-caste families in Karnataka being pressured to make their young daughters devadasis in order to 'please the gods' or impoverished farmers forced to sell their daughters into prostitution; from ageing, neglected widows voluntarily setting off to Vrindavan to disillusioned ex-revolutionaries turning to the trade in a desperate bid to survive, I saw how the lethal combination of poverty, patriarchy and religion often left women face to face with deep discrimination and abuse. And when the exploitation of women is veiled behind religious faith, the government and political parties too turn a blind eye to it.

In the face of this widespread problem, as I despaired about what my inconsequential news reports could possibly achieve, one of my articles* about devadasis being initiated in Uchangi had a much greater impact than was expected. Sabu Stephen from S.L. Foundation, Thiruvananthapuram, approached the Supreme Court with this article. All of a sudden, my article was moving ministries – the Karnataka Chief Secretary and the Central Ministry of Home Affairs were instructed to step in; the National Commission for Women would conduct a study in conjunction with the University of Madras. The case even caught the attention of the national media.

The court's intervention seemed to have been fruitful too; when I revisited Uchangi in February 2016, I couldn't see a single person initiating new devadasis.

While this was certainly no small victory, my travels were already showing me that very often interventions,

---

* 'What have we done to be made devadasis?'. *Malayala Manorama.* 2 February 2014.

even well-meaning ones, would not end oppression, only change its face. Even though the devadasi practice was banned in Karnataka back in 1982, the practice continues to this day. *Mujra* dancers forced out of Ujjain by the government simply ended up in Mumbai's Kamathipura. Even the banning of sati, lauded as a significant progressive step, had an adverse side effect. Many families began to abandon widows at temples, such as the Kalighat temple in Kolkata, turning these areas into hotbeds of prostitution.

The fact is that traditions and customs become deep-rooted in the minds of people and are difficult to reform. I have realized that the heritage that we take pride in is not necessarily prestigious for everyone. What is more unfortunate is that many have become so conditioned that they do not even realize they are being exploited. Even while devadasis proudly defended their patron goddess, or the widows in Vrindavan declared that they were content with their lives there as Lord Krishna's 'Radhas', it was obvious that most of them were unhappy with the hand that society had dealt them.

Researching for and writing this book has brought about a radical change in my perspectives on sex workers. The lives I saw made me reckon with arguments of sex work as labour and sex workers as eligible for labour rights. All the same, I got a clearer picture of the exploitation that exists in sex work as well. The disturbing images of Charu who learnt it was easier to subsist through sex work than get a better life through a revolution, Sandhya who took pride in not giving birth to a girl, and a number of other sex workers of Sonagachi and Kamathipura remain uneffaced in my mind.

In the end, I realize that a complete investigation is quite impossible. I have only documented what has been shared with me by the people I met, and what I have seen and experienced first-hand. I have tried my best to put aside my political leanings and moral standpoints to listen to everyone without prejudice or bias, sticking to journalistic ethics. I believe that the book reflects various viewpoints without fear or favour. One can only hope that this book increases awareness and perhaps helps in some small measure in improving the lives of so many.

# 1

# No More Dancing in Mangaluru

ON 25 SEPTEMBER 2008, ONE HEADLINE SCREAMED ACROSS most newspapers: 'Dance bars to be shut down in Mangaluru'. Obviously, the news became the talking point in the newsroom. Most of us journalists wanted to visit a dance bar before they were shut down. The Karnataka government's decision to approach the Supreme Court against the high court verdict not forbidding women dancers at bars in Mangaluru became the topic of discussion at the sub-editors' desk in Kannur, Kerala. The government had declared strict action on all illicitly run bars.

Our chief sub-editor, sitting aloof from our discussions, remarked nonchalantly, 'They are sure to continue illegally even after the ban.' This was true indeed. Our Mangaluru correspondent confirmed the bars would operate even after the ban. Our initial excitement waned. But then someone said, 'If dance bars are run illegally, that's precisely when we should go there. That will give us a story.'

The discussion was wrapped up for the time being. Such debates come up at the news desk almost every day, and sometimes the enthusiasm for discussing news stories would be just as short-lived as the news itself.

Several months later, however, I became engaged with dance bars once again, purely by chance. I began to ponder how I could get access inside the now-illegal dance bars. Some of my colleagues asked me to rethink whether such a story would be appropriate as it would affect the livelihoods of scores of people for whom dance bars were the only means of survival, albeit illegal. Rather, they suggested I focus on the rehabilitation of those rendered unemployed because of the ban. Such a perspective set me thinking. Neither the government nor society had made any provisions to rehabilitate those marginalized by the new laws, or incorporated them into development schemes. It began to dawn on me that the right way to do such a story would be to focus on those who had lost their means of sustenance.

Then, I came to know from various sources within the Karnataka police that several women who earlier danced in the bars had now resorted to prostitution. I felt the urge to visit the place personally to get a clearer picture. As often happens with leads like these, several other perspectives could emerge from the bylanes of a small story. I set off for

Mangaluru on a regular workday, when I was not too tied up with other stories.

Most visitors to Mangaluru follow a standard routine of heading to the Panambur beach, which is about 12 kilometres from the city. I too arrived at Panambur like a tourist and began my investigations at the line of autorickshaws parked adjacent to the beach. One face held my hopeful gaze. I felt intuitively that he could help me with some useful information and quickly boarded his rickshaw. Soon, the chatty driver Mani took up the role of a guide too.

'What is there to see other than this beach? Are the ladies who used to work in the dance bars available?' I asked him straight up.

'How many do you need, sir?' Mani asked. 'This is the only job for those women now.'

'Well,' I hesitated before adding on, 'what I actually need is to get some information.'

'Sir...' He became guarded, slowly bringing his auto to a halt. 'Are you a policeman?' He was suspicious now.

I laughed. 'No, I just want to know about their lives.'

Mani thought for a while, maybe assessing his risk in helping me. I began to regret asking him. It took me a long time to convince him I was not from the police and that my purpose was to study the lives of the bar dancers. If I had told him I was a journalist, that would have made him even more reluctant to open up.

He finally relented with a disclaimer. 'The hotel staff will not let you approach them and talk like that, sir. That would be a huge risk. You must go there as a customer. Then it is up to you to get any information you need.'

'That's all right. Let's get going,' I agreed.

'Sir, you are really not from the police, are you?' Mani asked me again, mistrust lodged deep in his mind. However, he started the rickshaw. 'Why on earth would you come to Mangaluru to learn about the women here when such ladies are available in Kerala too?' he asked, his doubts still not satisfied.

'I have come to Mangaluru after completing my research on the women in Kerala,' I attempted to explain.

He wasn't very convinced. 'I will drop you outside the hotel. You must go in on your own. I cannot help with anything else. If you turn out to be a policeman, they will finish me off.'

I flashed my best smile. 'Look at me. Do you really think I could be a policeman?'

He surveyed me from head to toe and finally seemed to be satisfied and free of his misgivings. The rickshaw stopped at Kodikkal, two kilometres from Mangaluru on the Panambur–Mangaluru highway. Pointing me towards a hotel, Mani told me to carry on. I gave him the fare and got off. An antiquated board outside the entrance read 'Hotel Prithvi Regency'. The four-storeyed building had the same ancient air about it. A young man sporting a long tilak on his forehead sat at the reception. He looked at me indifferently as I approached him. Unsure of how to begin, I stared back at him. He seemed to lose his patience and asked, 'Ladies?'

'Yes,' I responded with palpable relief.

He rang a bell. A young man with distinctly light eyes appeared out of nowhere. A wordless communication took place between them. The bellboy then asked me to get into the lift with him and pressed the button for the third floor.

'How old are the women?' I asked as soon as the lift doors closed.

'You can see all of them and pick whoever you want,' he said.

We arrived at the third floor. The lift opened up into a long hallway with rooms on either side. Some of the doors were closed, while half a dozen were open, with a woman behind each of them. Some looked too young to be called 'women'. There were a few younger girls huddled together in one room. The bellboy asked me to pick one from the many. As I entered each room, the women inside stood up to be inspected by me. I zeroed in on one who looked the oldest among them all. The bellboy seemed concerned. He called me outside and asked, 'Are you sure, sir? Aren't the younger ones better? We will arrange for a discounted rate if that is the problem.'

I refused his generosity on the offer and said I would stick to my decision. He smirked slightly and told me the rates. 'Seven hundred rupees for 15 minutes and twelve hundred for a full hour.'

'Shall I pay it to the lady?' I enquired.

'No,' he said and stretched out his hand. 'You need to pay me in cash.' I handed over the amount, which he promptly pocketed and went back to the lift. 'Please give her some tip,' he reminded me as the doors closed.

I entered the room. 'Close the door,' the woman smiled and told me. She looked to be about 45 and wore a traditional *lehenga* and blouse. She spoke the local dialect of Kannada, and although I wasn't very familiar with it, the dialect spoken in Mangaluru mixed several English words and was easy enough to follow.

As I closed the door, the lady opened a drawer and took out a condom. 'Please wear this,' she told me. I took the condom from her.

Divya was from Davanagere in Karnataka. I told her why I had come. She remained silent for a while, her face clouded with fear and doubt. She grimaced as she seemed to remember something and said, 'You can report that all those bar girls are now on roadsides and in hotels selling their bodies. Several other bar girls are in the other rooms. There are also others whose bodies have become so damaged that they are unfit for this business and wander about town. You can meet all of them and report to the government. But what is the government going to do? They can't do anything.' She was lost in her thoughts as anger and revulsion took over her face.

I sat quietly, taking in her bitter outburst. The room suddenly grew dense with the stifling smell of her perfume.

'How did someone from Davanagere end up here?' I asked her softly.

'I was made a devadasi when I was a child,' she responded. 'For a long time, I was the keep of a landlord in Davanagere. Soon enough, he got bored of me. Then someone brought me to Bengaluru, where I was taught to dance by a lady from Kolkata. I then joined a dance bar. After spending two years in that bar, another man brought me here. When dance bars were banned, we operated one here, illegally, for a while. But when it was shut down, I was forced to get into this field.'

I had only read about devadasis in stories of yore until then, so it was a shock to hear her say she had been one. My understanding was that devadasis were temple dancers who were historically accorded much respect and status in society. There was even a period when kings supposedly offered their daughters to temples as devadasis.

However, history tells us that during the period of the Brahmanical supremacy, devadasis had to yield to the wishes of the upper castes and thereby lost their revered standing in society. It was unimaginable that this inhumane custom, which set the backdrop for Achicharithams in Malayalam literature during 13–17 century CE, was still being practised.

Divya continued with her tale. 'My father did not have the means to raise or educate me, so he turned me into a devadasi. This was the standard practice. If people in our village did not have the means to bring up or marry off a daughter, she was offered as a devadasi at the temple on the first full moon in the month of *Magha* after she attained puberty. After that, the girl was forced to live her life as someone's keep. Some like me were fortunate enough to escape to Mumbai and Bengaluru. Others live wretched lives right there in the village temple and eventually die in misery.'

'Do they allow devadasis to be kept as keeps?'

'Of course. In fact, girls are turned into devadasis to be kept as mistresses in the first place. They are packed off when the men get bored of them.'

'Then why on earth would the family support this practice?'

She grew impatient with my naïveté. 'Our parents are unable to look after us. That's why we are turned into devadasis. They have no option but to support this. You must go to that place and see for yourself to know what it is like. Every house is in abject misery and starvation. If a girl is born amidst such poverty, what else can they do? It is an unbearable burden.'

'How can such practices exist even in this day and age?' I exclaimed in disbelief.

Divya laughed derisively. 'You know those Sri Ram Sena

people out there supposedly reforming this place? They are the same ones who give consent and support the offering of girls as devadasis during *Maghapournami* (the full moon night in the month of *Magha* of the Indian calendar). They say that the custom is necessary to placate the goddess in the village, whereas in the cities, they say prostitution is against the gods. They are such hypocrites!' she ranted.

'Does the Sri Ram Sena support the creation of devadasis?' I enquired.

Divya withdrew, fear palpable on her face. 'You must be from the Sri Ram Sena.' She grew worried. 'Are you here to provoke me into blaming the Sri Ram Sena and get me into their bad books?'

'No,' I assured her. 'I would like to know more about Davanagere, your hometown.'

'If you want to know more, you need to go to my town and ask around, not here. Go there and find out what the situation is,' she lashed out, clearly angry.

I felt that if I were to calm her down, I could get a clearer picture. But the chance had been missed. She refused to entertain any more questions, probably because she began to believe I was from the Sri Ram Sena. She did, however, divulge that the hotel staff pocketed 500 rupees from the 700 that was charged for their services, while they were given hardly 200.

Before I could extract any more information about Davanagere, there was a knock at the door. Divya got up and opened the door halfway. A male voice announced that my time was up. She told him something and locked the door behind her. 'Sir, if you would like to get on with things, please do what you have to do and move on.' She was now impatient to get rid of me.

She hadn't yet fathomed that I was not here to partake of the services she offered. 'What I want is information about your hometown,' I tried my luck again. But that only served to double her anger. She then went to the door, opened it and gestured for me to leave. I realized there was no point in asking her more questions. I tried to plead, but she grew evasive. So I quietly left the room. Inside the lift, I no longer thought about the bar dancers. Instead, I felt that the lives of Divya and others like her could not be reduced to a Sunday news magazine story. My mind was filled with the heartrending images of hundreds of miserable little girls being doomed to live their life as devadasis in some temple in Davanagere in Karnataka. Was this true? Would they end up in a seedy hotel room or on the dangerous streets?

I needed to know more. So I decided I had to go to Davanagere myself.

# 2

# The Dark Full Moon of Uchangi

THE CITY OF DAVANAGERE IS ON THE WESTERN SIDE OF Karnataka, about 265 kilometres from Bengaluru on NH4 and 284 kilometres from Mangaluru. Davanagere is also the headquarters of its eponymous district, which was formed when Chitradurga district was split up in 1997. The pilgrim centre of Uchangi is another 30 kilometres east of Davanagere. Uchangi was historically significant as the capital of the Pandya kings. I grew interested in this temple town when I read several newspaper accounts which reported that a Durga temple atop a hill here was a hotspot for devadasi initiation rituals. According to my friends in the Karnataka press, such activities continued unabated despite being legally banned.

I arrived in Davanagere on the day of the full moon in *Magha* along with three friends, scriptwriter KR Hari, Sibi from Kodungallur, and Rathish from Kodagu. Hari had come here earlier to see the *Maghapournami* festivities when he was an engineering student. Rathish was my translator, as it was essential to grasp the nuances of the dialect spoken in these interior areas. We hailed a cab to Uchangi right from the railway station itself. Our cab driver, Kumar, was delighted when we told him we had come all this way to pay our obeisance at the Durga temple hearing of its fame. As he grew more enthusiastic, the car seemed to accelerate further. Kumar regaled us with several tales of the temple. All his stories invariably had the same central theme of the goddess's unquestionable power.

The devadasi system was banned in Karnataka in 1982. However, the practice continued in Uchangi both covertly as well as openly. The orthodox refused to accept the ban, seeing it as an encroachment into tradition. This was clear from Kumar's words when he said, 'Bans exist only on paper. Can the government prohibit divine customs? No. That is why the system continues here with the blessings of goddess Uchangi. These matters are related to the culture of our village and cannot be ignored. The priests in the temple will vouch for it. They say that if the tradition is discontinued, our village will plunge into destruction, which is why they support it. Even the parents of the girls bring them voluntarily despite the ban. Who else but the mother-goddess is responsible for this? Laws are just an eyewash, sir; these things will continue. The government is also aware of this. They will have to pay heed to people's faith. How else can they get the votes that keep them in power?' he ended ominously.

We had covered half the journey, leaving behind Davanagere and several remote villages. Corn fields were on either side of the road, the dull yellowish hue of their leaves on the verge of fading. Scattered tree houses that were used as watchtowers were built in the middle of the fields, breaking the monotony. Once we crossed the maize fields, we could see clusters of small homes – some thatched, some tiled – dotting the landscape, which slowly gave way to vast expanses of sunflower fields. It appeared as though an entire ocean of yellow flowers had been torn asunder by a black tape – the road that seemed to stretch endlessly.

My heart sank as I surveyed the road. I felt that the taxi was not going quick enough for us to reach the temple by the evening. The timing was crucial to get a comprehensive view of the rituals that are related to the devadasi tradition. However, events later that evening made it clear as to how laws and bans become totally irrelevant when all sections of a society as well as the government jointly believe in retaining the status quo.

As we got closer to the temple, the roadside became more interesting. Groups of people were travelling with young girls in tow, who wore festive clothes, were bedecked in flowers and bore salvers that carried offerings to the deity. Older women with matted hair also accompanied them, instructing the younger girls to move aside when vehicles passed by. Some of the older women were also carrying offerings. 'These are the older jogammas (devadasis),' Kumar explained. 'The younger ones are to be initiated as new jogammas. The photo you see on the plates is of the goddess Uchangi.'

It seemed that the little girls had about them the mild curiosity of someone who had come to watch a festival from somewhere far away without actually participating in it. Only a few eyes betrayed the traces of what was to happen. The older women, on the other hand, had the air of being in control, directing every motion of the younger girls. There were several groups consisting of only old jogammas too.

Kumar then pointed to the distance and said, 'That is the Uchangi temple.' Beyond the sunflower fields was a hillock, atop which a small light was visible. It was quarter past six, and it was growing dark. I began to feel restless as I wished to take a picture of the temple in natural light. The road to the temple grew more and more crowded. Swarms of jogammas now descended on the road, their fervent but unfamiliar chants of '*uda, uda*' reverberating in the air.

It was nearly seven by the time we reached the valley that led to the temple. We had to cross a sunflower field through a dirt road before the uphill climb. By then, the cries of '*uda*' had become loud enough to drown out our conversations. We bid goodbye to Kumar and joined the crowd ascending the hill.

The Uchangi hill seemed to be a rocky fortress. The narrow pathway to the temple had been smoothened by the footsteps of the devotees over the ages, and it was punctuated here and there by an occasional step that was carved out of stone. Most of those climbing the hill were women. The few men were all dressed in saffron clothes. As we wore trousers, we were getting some unwanted attention. Higher up, vendors crowded both sides of the pathway and sold various coloured powders that were stacked in huge sacks. The colours, I learnt, were to be sprinkled on the girls who were to become jogammas after the rituals, just like on Holi. It is believed that sprinkling the colours on the girls would 'please' the new jogammas.

While watching the vendors, I suddenly sensed a rise in the tempo of the '*uda*' chants from behind me. The devotees began to move aside respectfully, their hands folded in piety. I saw a group of six to seven bare-chested men wearing dhotis and carrying a gold-coloured idol which was mounted on two golden poles. The devotees around me began to chant repeatedly, 'Uchangiamma, worship her.' When I took out the camera, the women and children around me looked amazed. They were probably seeing a camera for the first time in their lives.

The poles were then placed briefly on the ground while the priests conducted some purification rituals and distributed the *prasad*. The idol was once again hoisted on the men's shoulders and carried up to the temple. Cries of '*uda*' resumed with more intensity. The devotees were screaming, yearning for another glimpse of their goddess.

Once the procession left us behind, we made our way among the rocks to get a better view of the temple from the top. In the meantime, one of the saffron-clad men who had gone ahead had stopped and waited for us. He began speaking with us casually, in a friendly manner, but soon it was clear his primary objective was to find out why we had come. We asked him his name several times, but he avoided introducing himself. Moreover, he insisted there was nothing to see at the temple at this time and that we should come back the next morning.

We told him our purpose was to study the various traditions and rituals of the temple. We weren't sure if he believed us, but he was more willing to talk after that. We learnt that the word '*uda*' was a composite of 'Uchangi' and 'Durga'. In Kannada, he said, the word meant 'a plea to the goddess for protection'. He showed us the Uchangi fort and the *anehonde*, or the elephant pond, where elephants were bathed in earlier times. About an acre in size, the pond was built under the Nayaka dynasty. 'When you come here tomorrow morning, you will be amazed at the number of people who come here to bathe,' the man told us proudly. 'The water in this pond is sacred.'

Here, there was a signboard that read, 'The devadasi tradition has been legally banned from the year 1982.

Violators of the law will be subject to imprisonment and fines.' He walked ahead, totally ignoring the board. As we walked to the temple, a steady flow of devotees descended, most of them women with matted hair – the prevailing belief is that matted hair means the goddess had cursed those devadasis who had turned to prostitution.

'No more worship will happen up there tonight. Everyone is returning. When you come back tomorrow morning, the temple will be so crowded there will hardly be any standing room,' our guide exulted as he reiterated there was nothing worth seeing up there. Nonetheless, we decided to see this for ourselves. The man continued to follow us, so we decided to use him as our ad hoc guide to avoid further friction.

The temple was at the centre of a flat plateau about an acre wide. Its walls were built of rocks. A huge bell hung from an arch just outside. Inside, a stone-laid walkway had been built, sheltered under a concrete roof. The roof of the sanctum sanctorum had been paved with stone too. There were indeed very few people within the premises. However, jogammas emerged every now and then from below and headed towards the temple, sometimes by themselves, sometimes in groups accompanying young girls.

'Who are these girls coming up here with offerings?' I asked our guide. He tried to be evasive initially and said he did not know, then quickly came up with a satisfactory response. 'They are girls who recently started menstruating.

As per tradition, they have to pay obeisance to the goddess at night.'

Some of the jogammas who passed by smiled at him meaningfully. He gestured to them to take a seat a little further away. When another pair of jogammas made their way towards him, he stopped them and told them that he would come to them. He appeared to be rather harsh with some of the jogammas even as he took care to maintain a polite demeanour with us.

The bead chains worn by the jogammas were strikingly peculiar. Five beads in different colours were placed in the centre. Some of the chains carried a locket that had the goddess's picture embossed on it. Our guide explained such chains were given to jogammas after strenuous worship and thus had great powers.

Even the other ornaments worn by the jogammas were unique. Their arms were covered with green glass bangles all the way to their elbows. They wore brass anklets on one foot. Some of the salvers carried by the younger girls had the same kind of ornaments that were worn by older jogammas. I was quite certain these girls would be initiated as devadasis that same night.

Just then, another group of two younger women and an older jogamma, who didn't look more than 30, entered the temple and sat close to us. If the devadasi tradition had been discontinued as per the law, we asked ourselves, how could this woman become a jogamma? Surely the tradition continued here, we concluded. Seeing us discuss animatedly in our mother tongue, our guide got rather suspicious. When another saffron-clad older man arrived, they began to talk among themselves in low tones, after which the older man told us the remaining rituals were only for women. He asked us to go down as the presence of men would nullify the rituals being conducted. I wanted to counter by asking him why on earth he was present for the rituals then, but stopped myself as things could turn unpleasant.

We hesitatingly retraced our steps down the hill. Our guide looked on, just to make sure that we left. Down the path, we came upon a trader selling colours. 'Buy some colour, sir,' he asked us. 'Don't you want to put it on the devadasis tomorrow?'

'Aren't the colours meant for new devadasis?' I asked in all sincerity.

'Yes, sir, but you can apply colour on older ones as well. That is considered auspicious too,' he talked glibly, trying to get some business going.

'Will there be more devadasis here tomorrow?' I asked.

'Of course. Today is the *Magha* full moon. Why else do you think these girls have been brought here tonight? All the maidens who have gone into the temple tonight will become devadasis from tomorrow.'

'How does that happen?' I asked.

'Did you see the pond on your way up?' he asked. We said we hadn't. 'All the girls who went up today will be asked to bathe in the pond at midnight. Because it's a full moon night, it is special. The girls will be stripped naked for the ritual so that they can absorb the moon's rays in their entirety. Once they've received the blessings of the moon, they will be taken to the sanctum sanctorum, where they will be declared as devadasis. From thereon, they will become the temple's property.'

'Can't we watch the devadasi initiation rites?' I asked innocently.

'No way, sir!' the man replied vehemently. 'That is not allowed. When someone tried to view this in the past, they lost their sight!' I already knew about such fictitious warnings because of my friend, so I could not help stifle a laugh when I saw the fear on the man's face. But the vendor was not at all amused by our mirth, so we hastily bought some colour to placate him.

It was now past 8.30 p.m. The lights from the temple and the shops along the path blended with the moonlight and created a halo around the hilltop, rendering it impossible to see anything clearly in the valley below. It seemed pointless to wait any longer, so we made our way down to the sunflower fields, where everything seemed to be generously dusted in gold in the moonlight. We could see jogammas emerging in droves now. They would spend the night out in the open and make their way to the temple for *darshan* early next morning. We could see them trying to find spots along the roadside and among the rocks to rest for the night. Only a few of them were accompanied by men – and that too to provide security to the women. Some of the men approached the jogammas with an expression of awe. It appeared to me that if the jogammas were the servants of god, the men were the slaves of those servants. I thought it would be useful to talk to the jogammas directly. When I told them that I was a journalist from Kerala and had come here to understand their problems, several of the jogammas crowded around us with hopeful eyes. 'The government promised us a pension, but we haven't received anything yet,' the jogamma Radhamma complained bitterly. 'We have been ousted from our homes. Our families made us devadasis to get rid of us anyway. We sustained ourselves for a brief while on the temple. But we were expelled from there too. Now we have no home to call our own. If we were to get a pension, it would at least be enough for our medicines.'

'Don't you have children to take care of you?' I asked her.

'No, devadasis are not allowed to bear children,' she said. 'Don't you know we serve Mother Uchangi?' Her eyes gleamed in pride.

I spontaneously retorted, 'So has Mother Uchangi abandoned you now?'

Her pride hurt, Radhamma lashed out. 'Never! Mother has asked them to take care of us. It is the government that is not doing the needful. Why blame her for it?'

I tactfully changed the topic. 'How did your hair become matted like this?'

'That is because the Mother resides in it. This is her blessing. Not everyone is lucky enough to get it,' she replied proudly.

'Why are you in such misery despite such blessings?' I asked.

'The misery is man-made and has nothing to do with the goddess,' she retorted.

Eager to know more, I took a calculated gamble and asked her, 'Some people say matted hair is the curse of the Mother because you took to prostitution.'

As expected, Radhamma lost control and burst into colloquial invective in Kannada. 'Who the hell has been spreading such nonsense?' she screamed.

'Are you saying you are all virgins?' I asked her, lowering my tone.

'No,' she said, her civility back in place. 'We gave up our virginity to appease the goddess.'

'But there are several among you who go with other men,' I declared authoritatively.

Radhamma took on the air of a teacher as she explained, 'See, they ousted us from the temple, and thereafter, we were forced to become the mistresses of various people. The people in the temple cast us out after using us. How were we expected to live after that? Who would take us in? Only those who wanted our bodies would do so, and we had to compromise and live with them. What else could we do? Will journalists like you take care of us? Is the government taking care of us? How can you blame us for fending for ourselves?' She ended her tirade in frustration and anger.

'It is not the press or the government that is saying such things. It is the people inside the temple,' I said.

'What right do they have to judge us? Do you know who they keep in the temples? Only those women whose bodies they desire. Only those women. As simple as that. Once their lust is satiated, they avoid the women and throw them out. And now they have the nerve to blame it on us!' Radhamma's voice grew thick with indignation.

By now, several other jogammas had gathered around us. All of them had similar stories of misery to share – no one to take care of them in their old age and not having a roof over their heads. Yet, it felt strange to me that they took pride in being devadasis. I soon inferred from their conversations that certified devadasis received a pension, and the show of pride could be in the hopes of securing one.

A young woman then approached us and introduced herself as Ambika, a volunteer from the Devadasi Liberation Front. She told us she was there to make sure there were no attempts to turn young girls into devadasis, as it was an auspicious day for the sacred ritual. She said their volunteers were present at temples all over Karnataka wherever such events were likely to take place, such as in Saundatti and Bellary, and that because of their efforts over the past four or five years, such instances had greatly reduced. If they were to let their watch down, she said, the tradition would resume. They had come there as a group, and the volunteers were searching every part of the temple for suspicious cases.

'Have you been able to apprehend anyone red-handed?' I asked.

'About eight years ago, when we first volunteered, we had caught a few people. But later, as temples realized the power of our organization, they began to avoid these rituals,' Ambika explained. 'Nonetheless, now these rituals are conducted at home by replicating the ceremonies. I am sure this will be the case in several homes today. Unfortunately, we are not empowered enough to barge into homes and prevent this from happening.'

Obviously, there was a major discrepancy between what she said and what we had witnessed that day. Though Ambika talked about the struggles of the Devadasi Liberation Front, most of her statements ended by advising us to visit Harapanahalli to talk to Renuka, the president of the Front. 'She will tell you more.' We didn't want to counter her by telling her we had seen several young girls inside the temple that night, so we left it at that. It was close to midnight by now, and the full moon was at its luminous best. The jogammas were struggling to sleep. Long ago, they would have been brought to this hill on a full moon night such as this and decreed as devadasis. Since then, they had been fated to a life without light. Did the full moon remind them of the darkness within their lives? I asked myself.

The initiation rituals would have begun by now, but we couldn't see anything except the big lamps outside the temple. Another volunteer, a local man, from the Liberation Front came to us at that point. He told us he was actually a member of the Democratic Youth Federation of India (DYFI) and had joined the Front as he was drawn to its activities. He had come to see if anybody he knew had brought their daughters to the temple for the ritual, and he proudly affirmed he had not.

I told him about the children I had seen at the temple. 'Don't you think there is a high possibility the ritual will happen tonight?' I asked him.

'Truth is, upper-caste people would like the system to continue,' he said. 'For poorer families, it is a boon as they don't need to spend to marry off a girl child. The system is thus acceptable to all sections of society. Only the law is against it. You can imagine how feasible the implementation of such a law will be in such circumstances. Moreover, the BJP government cannot implement a strict ban as the Vishwa Hindu Parishad (VHP) and Bajrang Dal both support it. Will the BJP take a stand against them? The government machinery is merely a paper tiger. The police is present, but nothing comes of it. I am here to check only if anybody is forcefully bringing girls to the temple to push them into being devadasis against their wishes. Other than that, I have no intentions of intervening with those who come here voluntarily.'

His words told us even the Left in Karnataka, though it claimed to oppose the culture, had taken a soft and pragmatic approach to the practice. The Devadasi Liberation Front was probably under the control of Leftist organizations, and I thought that DYFI members had volunteered with the Front to strengthen their hold on the organization.

Our plan was to spend the night in the valley to see the early morning rituals. But our new friend from DYFI advised us that if we intended to watch the rituals, we had better change our clothes from trousers to the more acceptable saffron dhotis so as to not attract unwanted attention. This was the sensible thing to do. Thankfully, we had saffron dhotis with us, though not brought for this purpose explicitly. Nonetheless, they turned out to be helpful.

It wasn't yet 6 a.m. when a battalion of jogammas began to walk to the temple, rending the air abuzz with their orchestrated cries of '*uda, uda*'. The dirt path through the sunflower fields and into the valley was already crowded. Our reluctant guide from the previous day had definitely not been exaggerating. We could already see swarms of jogammas up the hill, advancing in a tearing hurry while chanting '*uda, uda*' rhythmically. All of them carried plates with offerings to the goddess – coconut halves, flowers, incense and colours. Some also had the goddess's picture with them. We joined the crowd of women, and thanks to our saffron attire, nobody stared at us. I mentally thanked our DYFI friend for his timely advice.

As the jogammas got closer to the temple, their pace increased and the chants got louder. When they entered the temple compound, they ran to the back of the temple and peeled the banana that was part of their offerings. The banana was then slapped with great force on the wall behind the goddess's idol. Several of the jogammas broke their bangles as they did this, but they did not seem too concerned. Most women hurried towards the wall and struck it with the banana as though in great fury. Squished fruit lay in a disgusting pile at the bottom, and many stepped in this pile of mashed bananas before adding their own fruit to it.

Here, we met the lawyer Abhijit, who stayed in the foothills and seemed like he could be an excellent source about the customs. On our way down, Abhijit showed us the *anehonde* pond, which was absolutely crammed with people. The jogammas bathed here before offering the bananas to the goddess, although the pond had pretty much dried up. I couldn't imagine how so many people could bathe in that pond, which was now nothing more than a puddle of murky water. Abhijit lived in an old house whose roof was covered in traditional tiles. He invited us to sit in its spacious veranda. His walls were filled with pictures of the goddess Uchangi in various sizes and shapes.

We could see jogammas getting ready in his backyard. Abhijit proudly explained that it was a tradition in their house to help devadasis and that hosting the devadasis was considered to be auspicious.

'Uchangi is an avatar of the goddess Durga who came to earth to destroy evil *asuras*,' Abhijit was clearly in his element once he opened the treasure chest of mythology. 'The Kadamba royal family built this temple more than 1,500 years ago. The Nayak royal family maintained the temple for a long time. The devadasi tradition was begun to appease the goddess. Now that the government has banned it, its ill effects will be borne by everyone. Can the government defeat the goddess?' When I hinted that it was only the upper-caste Hindus who were supporting devadasi culture to exploit them, Abhijit immediately corrected me. 'Who told you this nonsense? You can ask the poor. They are ready to turn their children into devadasis because it brings them great glory.'

'It is also alleged that the BJP and VHP support the devadasi system and ignore the law.'

'Never. These organizations work within the law. Some people have interfered with ceremonies that take place in homes. This is unacceptable. The Devadasi Liberation Front is not entitled to decide what rituals can be done at people's houses. Instead, they forcibly enter homes by alleging that girls are covertly being turned into devadasis. The VHP and Bajrang Dal might react to such trespassing,' he justified.

'Doesn't the law prohibit devadasi rituals even inside homes?'

'Yes, it does. But pujas can be conducted for a variety of reasons. So how can someone say the puja is for devadasis? These are personal matters, and no one should interfere with them. Volunteers of the Liberation Front complain to the police that such rituals happen inside homes. But the police have told them they cannot interfere in domestic issues. After all, there are limits to what the police can do,' he concluded.

We decided to switch to the topic of traditions. I asked him about the ritual of mashing bananas on the temple wall.

'That is called *hannu achuthu*. The belief is that the goddess's posterior should also be worshipped, which is why they cover the backside of her idol with mashed bananas and light incense. Uchangi Durga incarnated when an *asura*'s atrocities were getting unbearable. The *asura* was protected by a boon that he could not be killed by a weapon. So the goddess climbed the hill and urinated from that height. The force of the urine landing on the *asura*'s head killed him instantly. There are several such stories regarding goddess Uchangi.' Our lawyer-friend was upset that organizations stood against the goddess and the temple without respecting such beliefs and legends.

'Don't you think the Devadasi Liberation Front is doing a good job of rehabilitating senior jogammas?' we asked.

'The workers of the Liberation Front do not have

much social acceptance,' Abhijit said. 'They are being manipulated by others, and the sad part is they don't realize it.' We thought he was referring to the Communist Party of India (Marxist) or CPM, but his accusations were against someone else entirely. 'There is a pastor nearby who has taken it upon himself to rescue the devadasis. The Liberation Front supports him. But in reality, he is converting these helpless women to Christianity. They receive funds for conversion, so he can do it easily. The poor jogammas are quick to believe his words. He identifies women to convert with the help of the Liberation Front. Whoever they may think they are liberating, all they are doing is facilitating the conversion of Hindus into Christianity. How long can Hindus tolerate this?

'There have been several attacks against the pastor. The VHP and RSS are not to be blamed; Hindus anywhere will be provoked to action if they come to know of such activities. They do not need the backing of any organization. Moreover, what is wrong even if the RSS does attack in this situation?'

As the lawyer had begun to traverse the realms of right and wrong while defending fanaticism, we decided to wind up our conversation. As we emerged from his house after bidding him goodbye, we saw several jogammas coming down from the temple. We hurried towards them. Their grievances were all the same – rage at the officials who had denied them their pensions and their helplessness in indulging in prostitution.

Once the jogammas left, I wanted to meet the pastor. We walked to the main road and asked some of the auto drivers to take us to his house. But all of them turned out to be hardliners and refused outright. Now I was even more determined to visit him. Finally, an auto stopped by and agreed to take us there for a higher rate than usual.

By the time we finished the negotiations, it was nearly 10 a.m. We began chatting with our driver, who did not know the pastor's name but had heard his house had been attacked several times.

Before we could enquire more, we reached the house. It was only about 200 metres away from the junction and was a small, tiled construction that stood by itself. A simple-looking man sat in the veranda, wearing a white shirt and a pair of black trousers. Next to him sat a lady dressed in a sari. We alighted from the vehicle and walked inside the gate. The woman suddenly jumped up and asked us in Kannada who we were. We introduced ourselves as journalists from Kerala. Another young man wearing a lungi walked out. Then the man on the veranda asked us, 'Are you from the press?' He didn't look convinced.

The woman grumbled as she tied up her hair. The young man said something to her. The man on the veranda asked us to come and join him.

'Are you the pastor?' I asked.

'Yes.'

We sat down with him. The other two began to chide the pastor, asking him why he had invited us inside. We ignored them, while the pastor calmed them down by saying that Kerala newspapers were different than the ones in Karnataka. We immediately told the pastor we were here to investigate if the devadasi tradition was still being practised. This enthused him. 'You should write about these things. The Karnataka press is totally playing to the tunes of the BJP government. I'm sure several places would have initiated devadasis today.'

'Didn't you investigate?' we asked him.

'No. I have been threatened for my work, and I cannot investigate independently. As it is, the RSS has attacked this house several times. Who knows what they will do if I set out to investigate?' He justified his inaction. 'It is useless to go to the temple and monitor those who come for the ceremony. You cannot do anything to save the girls there. You should have gone to the homes of these poor people in the interior parts of the state. Then you could have identified the girls who were being prepared to become jogammas. You should have come here a week in advance. Not just here, the devadasi culture is strong in Bellary district too. You should go there and see for yourself. All those who live in poverty will be waiting for this day to turn their daughters into devadasis. The girls escape from the horrors of poverty temporarily, but three or four years later, they are forced to turn to prostitution for survival. Their lives continue to be financially insecure. And I am not talking about one or two people here.' The pastor ended his passionate lecture on that gloomy note.

We were aware this was not about one or two women. After all, we had seen the many jogammas and younger girls at the temple. 'Hasn't the government taken measures to give them pension?' I asked.

'That is just hogwash,' the pastor replied. 'Most of them have not received anything. If the devadasis have to get pension, they have to be listed in the register first, which won't happen unless the officials are placated. This is the situation.'

'What have you been doing for them?'

'I arrange for money that helps them get bare essentials like food and clothing. After all, that is what really matters,' he said conscientiously.

'What about the allegations that you have been converting them to Christianity?'

'Never!' he vehemently denied. 'We never force anyone to join our religion. But some people are attracted by our policies and approach us willingly. What can we do about that?' said the pastor.

I wondered if instead of rescuing children from being turned into devadasis, the pastor was simply exploiting their poverty. His agenda was simple, though covert –

adding to his flock of believers. In essence, he was only fishing in troubled waters.

The woman, though, did not like our questions about conversion. She came up to us and declared there was nothing more to talk about and commanded us to leave. There was no point in staying as the pastor had also fallen silent. I signalled the others to leave. Just then, the young man asked for our identity cards. I felt it would be better to clear his suspicions and gave him my card. He examined it with the precision of a detective. When I felt he had studied it thoroughly, I asked for it back. But strangely, he now asked us to stay for tea.

I hardly had the time to suspect his motives when a police van careened to a stop outside the gate. Several police officials charged in, some jumping over the fence in a hurry. The policeman who came in through the open gate held a gun in his hand. He stepped into the veranda and took my identity card from the young man and inspected it.

'Journalist?' he asked me as he cross-checked my face with the photo on the card several times.

'Yes,' I replied.

A smile spread across his face slowly, a smile of relief. I looked at his name plate and realized he was an SI. 'You guys gave us a scare,' he said, now laughing. 'We were told that an RSS group had come here to attack the pastor.'

The young man slowly slunk away, his head lowered.

But he could not be blamed. We laughed at our stupidity in turning up at the pastor's wearing the saffron dhotis.

I asked him about the devadasi rituals at the temple, but he denied any such incidents in areas under his jurisdiction. He bragged theatrically that people would not try anything while he was in charge and he was sorry to deprive us of a good news scoop. But he did not forget to mention we might get to see what we wanted in Harapanahalli. I remembered that Ambika had told us about the town the previous day as well. Harapanahalli was the centre of the Devadasi Liberation Front, so I decided to go and meet Ms Renuka, who was the state president of the organization. We hired the same van as earlier to drive to Harapanahalli. Here, instead of the sunflower fields, bleached cotton fields greeted us. The highway was occasionally bordered by ragi and mustard fields, and one could see tree houses intermittently. Most settlements along the road consisted of small, thatched huts, with a few that had tiled roofs. There were no concrete houses to be seen anywhere. Curiously, almost all the houses had something written on their walls in charcoal. I stopped our vehicle to have a closer look. The scribbles read 'Go today and come back tomorrow' in Kannada.

I asked one of the residents what it meant. He told me the scribble was to scare away ghosts. Apparently, ghosts were troubling the village a lot, and the writing was meant to deter the ghosts from entering the homes. The ghosts would read the scribbles and go back. When they returned the next day, the situation would be the same. The charcoal with which the words had been scribbled had innate powers due to a puja being conducted on them, the resident explained.

We were stunned. In a land where ghosts can read and write, no amount of absurdity is surprising!

# 3

# The Women Warriors of Harapanahalli

HARAPANAHALLI IS A TALUK HEADQUARTER IN DAVANAGERE district. Renuka lived in a colony near town, and when we arrived at her place at around 3 p.m., we could see several women who looked like jogammas on the street leading to the colony.

A wearied-looking lady answered the door. We were surprised when she introduced herself as Renuka. We hadn't expected a woman with such an exhausted demeanour. She explained that she had been wandering about in different places for the past few days. 'Little girls are being turned into devadasis in several places even now. Unless we are alert, we will not be able to identify such cases. Several other volunteers of the Front have been patrolling these areas day and night to make sure there are no new devadasis being initiated anywhere,' she said passionately.

Since she appeared to be too exhausted to talk, we asked her if we could return the next morning. She agreed. The next morning, she promptly called us. We reached her house by 10 a.m. Apart from the veranda, the house, although big compared to the others in the neighbourhood, had only one room and a kitchen.

Renuka had put out a grass mat for us to sit on the veranda. She told us humbly this was all the comfort she could offer. She then sat across us with a bag that was stuffed with numerous pamphlets and write-ups about the Front. As she took out the contents one by one and started explaining, I stopped her. 'I want to listen to your story, not the organization's,' I said.

'My story?' She seemed taken aback and curious at the same time. 'My story is no different story than that of the other jogammas.'

I requested her to tell her story so that we could understand the jogammas. She was quiet for a while. Then she started digging into her memories and told us about her life.

Renuka's family came from Sendur village in Bellary, a land of prosperous cornfields. But her childhood was too miserable to enjoy those bountiful fields. 'My parents were daily wage labourers, and the pittance they brought in was hardly enough for us to have ragi gruel twice a day. Do you know what my biggest dream was in childhood? To have two dosas for breakfast! We were only allowed that indulgence once in five months. We really did not have many dreams or desires in our childhood. This was the case with all the children in the Valmiki community, to which I belonged.'

The Valmiki community is a Dalit community who mostly worked as labourers in the fields belonging to the landlords. The feudal system continued to prevail in Karnataka's villages, and the Valmikis were people who were dehumanized because of the caste system. Renuka continued, 'In those days there was no work available to us other than agricultural work. All the land belonged to upper-caste families such as the Iyengars. Ragi and corn were the main crops. Most landlords owned more than a hundred acres.'

When she was a child, Renuka accompanied her father to the places he worked at, where workers would be served water in coconut shells. A steel vessel with water was set aside for the supervisors. 'I used to look longingly at them when they drank water from the steel vessel as I assumed that water would be sweeter. One of my childhood dreams was to drink water from a steel vessel like that.' When her father carried the ragi to their landlord's house, Renuka could see a brass vessel kept in a corner, an old and dirty vessel that had fungus on it. 'Even now, when I think of my childhood, the first image that comes to mind is of the vessel, which was kept upturned in the veranda outside the kitchen. No one took it inside even at night. The fate of that vessel was similar to us lower-caste people, who were denied entry into their landlords' homes.'

Renuka was admitted into school when she was six or seven. One advantage of going to school was that she got more gruel than at home. 'I did not know at the time that it was essential to study well to get a good job. But even if I had known that, I would not have studied as we children of lower castes assumed all the good jobs were kept aside for higher castes, while we went to school only for the gruel. We were least bothered about our studies. But one huge relief was that we were not discriminated against in school like elsewhere.

'The school was not segregated, and the venom of caste discrimination was yet to sink into the minds of other children. There were other schools where children from the Valmiki community were seated separately. But thankfully, we got lucky in that respect. Outside school, however, it was terrible. People from our community were served tea in coconut shells at teashops. I still remember how a tea shop owner was thrashed by Iyengars for serving tea in a glass cup to a stranger who happened to be from our community. Not that the incident affected me – we were too poor to even afford tea at the shop. We would manage to drink black tea only during the harvest season. If the harvest was good, we would get extra corn and ragi along with wages, which would be sold to buy provisions. If anything was left, we would buy tea that would last us for a week. This was how everyone around us lived, so we never thought much of it. The landlords were the only families who were well off in the village, and we understood quite early in life that we could not even dream of being like them.'

Because studying was never a priority, Renuka and others like her would just take what they needed from school – which was the free lunch – and then leave. On the day when their mother had to go to work, she or her older sister, Padmavati, would not go to school. They would babysit their younger sister, Sambovi, and do other household chores. 'Since I never thought that schooling was more important than my free lunch, I had no regrets in not going to school. Moreover, if mother went to work, we would replace gruel with rice for at least one meal. My only misgiving was about missing playtime at school. The only books I had were the free ones given to us by the school. At that point, I did not know books were valuable enough to be bought for money. Still, I did manage to study something. By the time I was in the fourth standard, I had begun to view my studies a lot more responsibly. Not that I had any big dreams, but since we were going to school anyway, I thought, why not pay attention in my classes?

'In the meantime, Padmavati, who had quit school when she was fourteen, began to receive wedding proposals. For families like ours, where daily sustenance was a struggle, it was impossible to keep a girl unmarried at home beyond that age. Valmiki families poorer than ours and who had no means to pay a dowry would start thinking about making the girl a devadasi.

'Once a girl is made a devadasi, she does not have to be married off, which is a big relief to the parents. Moreover, the girl becomes the property of the society once she becomes a devadasi. In some cases where the family is not inclined to do so, girls are sometimes forcibly turned into devadasis by the villagers in the name of belief and faith. Such things are easily done, unquestioned and unresisted, in villages caught up in superstitions. A temple oracle, known as *devarkal* in local parlance, would be used for this. It is believed that the *devarkal* is enlightened by God's will and is entitled to reveal to others what God wants, from time to time. But whose wishes do they really convey in the name of god? It is mostly their own wishes or those of the upper-caste folks. Our friend Durga was turned into a devadasi in this manner. She was a beautiful girl, and the wealthy landlords of the area wanted to make her a devadasi. After she attained puberty, Durga's brother fell ill, and this made things easy for the landlords. They declared the illness was ample proof of the goddess's anger towards the family. The solution was to offer Durga as a devadasi! The landlords and the oracle together dispensed the crime and the verdict in one go. Durga's distraught family had no choice but to agree. This is not just the story of one Durga, but of several others like her.' Thankfully, Renuka's sister Padmavati did not have to suffer the same fate. She was married off when Renuka was in the seventh grade, which she failed. Although the prime motivation to go to school had been the free gruel, her parents decided to not send Renuka to school any more. Someone had to take up the responsibility of domestic chores, and it fell on Renuka to assume those duties. 'That was the end of the school chapter.'

Despite my scant knowledge of Kannada, I could follow Renuka well because of her profuse gesticulations. Renuka was a fine storyteller, perhaps because of the numerous public speaking opportunities on behalf of the Liberation Front. Her words were precise and forceful.

By then, some workers of the Front had also joined us. Renuka continued her story. 'We moved to Adisamimatta in Harapanahalli after my sister's wedding. In those days, Harapanahalli was also where many women who had been forced to become devadasis lived. The situation was so bad that once a girl turned fifteen, her family had no choice but to turn her into a devadasi. She would be declared the temple's property. Even worse, the girls were forced to beg at the temple, which they considered a privilege. The more beautiful ones would be sought out by someone from the dominant castes, enticing them with money. For the hapless girls, who were struggling to scrape together two meals a day, anyone who offered them money for three straight meals was naturally a saviour. So they would be ready to do anything demanded by these "gods". In those days small thatched rooms called *puras* were attached to the temples, which were removed after the ban. Wealthy village landlords would rent out these rooms and allow their favourite devadasis to stay there, visiting them at will. Most devadasis who were regarded as servants of god during the day were nothing but slaves of the village lords at night. Not that the devadasis saw anything wrong in it. After all, one needs food to stay alive. The unspoken tradition was that once a devadasi was chosen by a rich man, she would not have to resort to begging. If she did, it would reflect badly on the landlord. He would therefore provide for all her needs. There were several instances where young girls who had not attained puberty were forced into this custom. The rich man's need was paramount, and age did not matter. The harrowing cries of so many innocent children have been buried in the walls of the *puras*. Eventually, the landlord would find the next devadasi after his former paramour grew older, and then she would be shunted out. After that, the *puras* would be closed for her. She would have to go back to begging within the temple walls. If, by chance, another landlord was attracted to her, he would become her next god. At times the new lord might want to show off and give her more comforts than the previous one. But this script had the same ending every time. Once he found a new devadasi, the former would be cast away. Then it was time for her to go begging.

'Soon enough, devadasis would get degraded to the status of regular prostitutes. They would become so desperate for survival that they would go with anyone who desired them. Truth be told, the devadasi custom is really a sort of prostitution centred around the temples. Sooner or later the devadasis exhaust their regular clientele who frequent the temples and have to move to the streets in search of new "gods". From then on, they become a sex worker on the streets.

'All of this was new to me. School seemed like a wonderful escape route from these realities. I could not free my mind, however; each devadasi girl I saw brought fear in me. And yet, somehow I did not think my fate could be similar too. The truth was that I was not willing to accept the undeniable reality.

'As soon as I attained puberty, people started frequenting our house to say that I should be made a devadasi. Landlords tried to persuade my parents by telling them it would be auspicious for the family and prosperous for the village. As a result, my family started thinking along those lines too. After all, that was the custom. Moreover, we were yet to repay the debts from my sister's wedding. Naturally, my parents must have thought it was better to avoid the additional burden of my wedding. However, it was impossible for me to give in to their plan, having seen for myself the horrors of the life of the devadasis. I made up my mind to not give in to them no matter the consequences and created a ruckus at home. My family stopped pressurizing me. But that was not the end.

'My sister would tell me that I was beautiful, although dark. Landlords and their acolytes would come home and say, "Won't our goddess be angry if you don't dedicate such a beautiful girl to her?" My parents would look at me helplessly, but I stayed firm in my resolve. The men would then abuse my parents and leave. Then I fell ill with typhoid, although no one knew it was typhoid in those days. We didn't have access to good treatment. When I was bedridden for more than four days, the landlords returned with the oracle. "The goddess has started getting angry," the oracle pronounced. "This is what happens if you don't dedicate beautiful girls to her. Now this disease will spread all over the village. Do you want the whole village to die because of your arrogance?" he asked ominously.

'Listening to this, my parents were petrified. In a way, I was also scared. But that did not mean I was ready to give in to them. I cared more about not having a miserable life than the tears of the villagers. Being a devadasi would mean that I would also end up as a sex worker like most of them. I was consumed by this fear. But my illness refused to subside. The landlords returned once more with the oracle, and this time their words had a threatening tone. I ignored them. But by then, the villagers had turned against me. They were afraid that the disease would put all of them in peril, like the oracle predicted. They could not understand why I would not agree. I was called an arrogant girl who had doomed the whole village selfishly. When I heard from several quarters that my family was going to be isolated, my resolve melted. Finally, I agreed to become a devadasi. But I set out conditions. I told them I would beg in the temple, as was the custom, and do the odd job. But I would not put up with anything beyond that. My family agreed. All they cared about was to allay the goddess's anger.

'I thus became a devadasi, albeit reluctantly. The rituals were done at home. Just like at the temple, our veranda was readied for the puja. Flowers were collected. The chain of beads that a devadasi wears was prepared. When the day came, the women in the neighbourhood first gave me a ritual bath at the well. I was then taken to the puja in the same wet clothes. A pedestal had been prepared and decorated with flowers, and I sat there while the puja was conducted. Many women had assembled to attend the rites. A picture of goddess Yellamma, the chief deity of the devadasis here, presided over the proceedings. At the end of the rituals, I was given a consecrated chain to wear. I was now a devadasi. I had heard that when the ritual was done at the temple, the girl would have to be totally naked. Thankfully, that was not the case at home.

'As a devadasi, I first begged at the temple. I would carry water to the temple and do other odd jobs to make the money that was required for my sustenance. I would come home to spend the night. Other devadasis were not so lucky. They did not have the option of going home as they had been abandoned by their families. This made things easy for predators. If the women were offered a place to sleep, they would be up for anything. Tired as they were after a day of begging and working at the temple, all they wanted was a bed for the night. The landlords took advantage of that. Only I returned home and slept, although not peacefully because my mind was always troubled by the pathetic condition of the other devadasis.

'At that point, I had not thought of protesting against the practice. For a long time, I was simply relieved I had escaped their fate. But soon, people began to approach me too. Their "advice" was that I should stay in the temple to ensure I had genuinely pleased the goddess. They sent other devadasis to advise me. I refused to be influenced and insisted firmly that I would go home at the risk of missing the goddess's beneficence.

'Most devadasis were discontent with their lives. But at the same time, they also wanted to make the most of the opportunity by serving rich men. They knew that once fresh meat was available, they would be abandoned. Hence, egged on by their families, they would constantly be working on new ways to keep the men under their sway. In the afternoons, when there was no work in the temple, this would be the main topic of discussion for the devadasis.

'Once, devadasis were chaste women who only enjoyed the company of one man at a time. In spite of the opportunities, they refused to surrender their bodies to anyone else and stayed true. It was only when they were replaced that they would consider fresh proposals for their companionship. Later, when they were abandoned and the temple rooms became unavailable to them, they moved to the streets. There were some, however, who escaped the high-handedness of the landlords.

'I knew one such woman, Parvati. She had been married off by her family at the age of nine. Her husband, a much older man, died within two weeks of the wedding. Parvati was sent back home. She attained puberty only two years after that. People began to eye her and told her family she should be made a devadasi. "This girl is meant to be a devadasi. Isn't that why god called her husband back even though she got married?" they said. The *devarkal* colluded with the gods and pronounced the same verdict. Parvati could not withstand the pressure, and became a devadasi. But even then, she did not pay heed to the landlords' demands. She finished all the chores at the temple and returned home. All invites to the *pura*s were declined. But the landlords wanted to have her at any cost. So they came up with new ploys, saying it was inappropriate of her to go home at night. "Her husband is dead. If she defies her fate and sleeps at home, the family will face the next death," threatened the *devarkal*.

'Thus, they got her own family to shut their doors on her. The landlords thought she would turn to them in helplessness. But Parvati was determined to fight back. She quit begging at the temple and washed the dishes at a tea shop in town. No one knew about her life at the tea shop. She worked there for a while before moving on to other jobs. As she was ready to do any kind of work, there was no paucity of jobs. This is how Parvati defeated the evil designs of the landlords.'

I noticed the pride in Renuka's eyes as she finished Parvati's story. That a woman could single-handedly challenge such a powerful system and take charge of her life, that too several years in the past, came as a great surprise to me. Renuka then told us about other devadasis.

'Like Parvati, Neelamma also had something of a success story. Neelamma was our neighbour who was turned into a devadasi when she was ten. A Harapanahalli landlord kept her for a while. A baby boy was born of that relationship. Now, a devadasi's child is discriminated worse than the lower castes. The child is denied the right to know who the father is. The devadasi is not allowed to reveal it either. Neelamma brought up her son as per these conventions. The upper castes believed children were born to devadasis as a result of divine wrath. Thus the child has to put up with such nonsense. Today, there are more than 10,000 such children in just two or three districts of Karnataka – children who do not know their fathers and are doomed to humiliation and isolation all their lives.

'Once the child was born, the landlord abandoned

Neelamma. She refused to take on another man. Life then became extremely hard for the mother and son. She put up a small shop in the village, but no one was ready to buy anything from a Valmiki, that too a devadasi who had sinned. Some people then advised her to start selling hooch. Neelamma had no other option, so she teamed up with them and started selling hooch in small plastic packets. These packets were immersed in water in tar barrels. When the police came to check, it seemed like a regular shop. Her business was run in this manner. Most of her customers would be agricultural labourers, and at times, young people from higher castes would also come. Even in those days alcohol had a way of erasing all caste barriers.

'Neelamma really did not have any other option. Though the money she got from selling hooch was meagre, she was determined to educate her son, Mohan. She enrolled him in school at the age of five, even though the tag of being a devadasi's son remained a burden for him. Such children were treated as accursed even by educated people, and they feared to let other children mingle with them.

'Neelamma then switched careers and became a daily labourer. She struggled to make ends meet but ensured that her son remained in school. Typically, people from the Valmiki caste become labourers right after high school. But Neelamma changed all of that. She sent him to college, and Mohan imbibed his mother's aspirations and worked hard, passing with flying colours from college. He completed a course in law at the Davanagere Law College and is now practising at the Harapanahalli District Court. He supports the Liberation Front with whatever legal advice we need. More than anything else, he is a stellar example for the children of our community.

'The privileged castes cannot stomach it when a lower-caste person climbs the ladder of success. There are orchestrated efforts at every stage to discriminate and demoralize them. There are tea shops in Davanagere even today that serve tea in coconut shells to lower-caste members. This is the same village that cut off the nose of a lower-caste man because he dared to visit a barber shop for a shave.

'I had always felt that our protests would be ineffective without the backing of an organization. The CPM then gave us the opportunity. They said their women's welfare branch – the Janavadi Mahila Group – would work for the welfare of devadasis and asked us to join them. I thought it was a good idea. We started planning joint programmes and working together. As time passed, we felt we needed a separate body to highlight our unique concerns. The CPM leadership also agreed to this, and so the Liberation Front came into being. The Janavadi Mahila Group continues to back us.

'We have been moderately successful in securing pensions and other benefits for devadasis. The government had commissioned a survey in 2004 to identify those eligible for pension. But officials belonging to upper castes couldn't let that happen. When the survey results came out, it said there were only 23,000 devadasis in Karnataka, which was far too low by our calculations.

'When I saw that list, I felt that the Front's struggles had regressed to where they began. However, we decided to press forward without getting disappointed. We had already scrutinized the foul play in the count. As per the government, only the districts of Bellary, Bidar, Gulbarga, Raichur, Koppal, Hubli, Belgaum and a few others had devadasis. If that was to be believed, who were the rest of us? We then organized ourselves into concerted protests. We demanded that a re-survey should happen in districts such as Davanagere, Chitradurga, Shimoga and Haveri. We challenged the government that we could conduct the survey more efficiently if the government did not have the resources for a foolproof survey. Volunteers of the Liberation Front then took over the survey and took to the streets, combing each and every nook and cranny for devadasis.

'We counted 55,000 devadasis in these four taluks alone. Several devadasis might have escaped to metros such as Bengaluru, Mangaluru and Mumbai. Though the ones who had moved to the metros may not need pensions, I was quite sure they too were doing sex work. The Devadasi Liberation Front believes there are nearly 83,000 devadasis in all of Karnataka.

'It wasn't difficult for us to identify the devadasis. Their living conditions were really distressing, especially in places like Halliya, where they hardly get food to eat and are forced to walk the streets looking for customers. Most women there are afflicted with HIV/AIDS too.

'A majority of the devadasis are also addicted to alcohol. When most of them turned to prostitution, they were already mentally exhausted. There are many who have mental problems, unable to disentangle themselves from the evil grip of alcohol and ganja. We were shocked to learn in our survey that 30 per cent of devadasis were alcoholics. The others abstained only because they could not afford intoxicants. Even when Neelamma was selling hooch, her regular clientele included several devadasis.'

I couldn't help ask Renuka about what I had witnessed at Uchangi Durga temple. 'Don't you think unless measures are taken to prevent new devadasis from being inducted, there won't be a permanent solution?'

Renuka agreed. 'Our organization has been staunchly protesting the practice of inducting new girls as devadasis. Though the practice was banned in 1982, it has covertly continued in several places. The government has put up boards at all temples where it was practised, but there are traditionalists everywhere who argue the practice is necessary for the land's welfare. They are the ones who secretly arrange these rituals. We have started intervening strongly in such areas. Threats are countered with threats.

When we learn that conservatives have threatened the poor with divine wrath, we go to those homes and warn them about the legal repercussions of going ahead with such practices.

'The truth is, most people did not know the practice had been banned by law until recently. When we tell them, they withdraw from the idea. Our interventions check any such forceful induction of girls as devadasis. Left-leaning organizations in Davanagere and Harapanahalli inform us in advance when they hear about such rituals. Based on their information, we go talk to the parents.

'The family usually contends that their daughters will be assured of three meals a day when they become devadasis. They pretend to be unaware of the dark future that awaits the girls. When the devadasis from the Front talk about their terrible experiences, the girls refuse their parents' plans. But those who wish to perpetuate the system bide their time till the girls attain puberty or fall sick to call on them with their ominous predictions. Though we outnumber them, they have the backing of faith. The words of those pretending to be god's allies are obviously more valued than those of the sacrilegious.

'We don't get timely information about temples, however. Nonetheless, we have managed to ensure the presence of the police in temple premises during the month of *Magha*, when these activities are at their peak. If we see any families with young girls, our volunteers tell them that the rituals in the temple are being recorded and that they will be arrested as soon as they come out. We need the police, but often the policemen themselves are upper-caste men or minions who favour the custom. It is most difficult in regions where the BJP and RSS are dominant. Ultimately, we can only dissuade the people. How do we stop those who are ready to sell their daughters? They remain unfazed when we threaten them with legal consequences. They will find the means to conduct the proceedings secretly.'

I couldn't hide my disbelief at Renuka's tales. There was so much to take in. In her words, the devadasi system continued to be practised in many parts of Karnataka despite the legal ban. There was widespread societal support too, either in the name of faith or through coercion. So I asked her how the Front could work despite so much opposition.

Renuka then told us about the 21-year-old Chandrika from Ambedkar colony, whose parents were coerced to make her a devadasi after she cleared grade 10. 'Because Chandrika was beautiful, the upper castes in her village approached her parents despite the legal ban. We talked to her parents and told them about the legal consequences. But the landlords countered this by advising them to conduct the ceremony inside a locked house so that no one would find out. Unless they did this, her parents were told, they would face divine consequences. The Front was in a quandary. We couldn't rescue her from a locked house. The plan was to shift her immediately after the ceremony to one of the rooms attached to the temple. We decided to approach Chandrika personally and tell her about the dangers that lay ahead. Her neighbours arranged the meeting for us. That's when we realized Chandrika was caught in a bigger quandary. She was in love with a young man and wished to marry him. She didn't know how to avoid this crisis, but for us, this was an unexpected blessing. We immediately contacted the young man, who was despondent about losing the girl of his dreams. Once we were convinced he was a good man, we decided we would get the two married off. His despondency gave way to strength when he realized we would back him.

'We then told Chandrika to prepare for her wedding. The girl was ecstatic, but her parents refused in fear of the goddess's anger. We convinced them that these were superstitions being forced on them. Their next worry was the dowry. But this was not a problem since the young man had assured us he did not want any. The parents finally agreed, and the marriage was held under the auspices of the Tahsildar at the registrar's office in April 2011. Members from the Front as well as office-bearers from the women's organizations acted as witnesses. We had pooled in some money to buy a few gifts for them. But in a way, we couldn't give her a better gift than the life we had helped her secure,' Renuka ended on a happy note.

Renuka told us that the biggest headache for poorer families is to marry off their girls, which is why female foeticide remains a big issue in Karnataka even today. 'Doctors use codes like Krishna (for a boy) and Lakshmi (for a girl) during illegally conducted gender tests. For those who don't want a Lakshmi, the liability is taken care of with a little more money. If not, the baby is abandoned after birth.'

'How far has the Front been able to intervene in the issue of caste discrimination?' I asked.

'Caste discrimination remains entrenched here even today. All in the administrative machinery join hands to isolate the lower-caste people. The attempt to cover up the molestation of a girl belonging to Samagara caste was part of this. The incident took place four years ago. The girl's upper-caste neighbour started making advances on her and when she resisted, raped her. Though she told her mother, the latter cried to her neighbours but did nothing else. When we heard this, we lodged a complaint at the local police station. But the police tried their best to get the case thrown out. The mother's concern, as usual, was that her daughter would not get a good match if she went ahead with the case. We decided the best solution was for the accused to marry the girl. After a bit of convincing, he and his family gave in to our pressure and agreed. Today, they live together happily as a family.' There was no point in asking her about the injustice in letting the offender marry the victim.

Renuka said that girls from backward communities silently endured all kinds of oppression. Because there was now a dearth of lower-caste girls who willingly became devadasis, people would intentionally ruin their marriage prospects. The parents, unable to bear the burden of an unmarried girl, would reluctantly agree to turn her into a devadasi. 'Our strategy is to keep fighting against such people till the police act on our complaints,' Renuka said. She then told us about other areas the Front and the Janavadi Mahila Group were involved in, so I asked her, 'Is the CPM intervening aggressively to stop the custom itself? Or are they only interested in the welfare of the devadasis?'

'They are involved in both areas,' Renuka said. 'As a political party, the CPM cannot interfere directly in this issue. Hence, we front the action. They are, however, active in rehabilitating devadasis. The party gives us full support in all our strikes and protests.'

I couldn't help but feel she was an instrument in the hands of the party. Although the CPM supported the devadasis in their efforts to get a pension, I felt that they should have also focused on providing education to younger women in high-risk areas to ensure they did not fall prey to this heinous practice. But I got a sense that their agenda was to capture the older devadasis' considerable vote bank, which the younger group would not be able to provide. While one party preserved their vote bank among the upper-caste Hindus by covertly supporting an undesirable practice, the other was similarly targeting their vote bank by narrowing their scope of action to providing pension for the suffering devadasis.

By now it was clear that neither the Congress nor the BJP, who ruled the state at the time, had done anything beyond putting a legal ban on the practice. They hadn't focused on any economic and social welfare measures that would allow impoverished communities to not be victimized by such evil customs. To me, this was the real reason behind the continuation of the practice. However, it was pointless to argue with Renuka on this. I also had to see for myself the situation in areas where the Front was not at all active.

'Go to Kudligi, Bijapur and Saundatti and you can witness it personally,' Renuka advised us. 'There some people don't even know devadasis are given pension, whereas here we are fighting for a raise in the pension amount.'

Several other women, all office-bearers, had arrived by now and were getting impatient to speak with Renuka. So we left her to her organizational duties and charted out our next destination.

# 4

# Rehabilitation Drama in Kudligi

KUDLIGI, WHICH FALLS BETWEEN THE TOURIST DESTINATION Hospet and Bengaluru, is quite well known for its devadasi tradition. I had heard from reliable sources that the town also hosted many sex workers, and I wanted to talk to them. My friend Pramod, who works in the BSF and was conversant in the local language, decided to accompany me.

Kudligi is about 280 kilometres from Bengaluru, on the Bengaluru–Hospet–Solapur road. It has come to be known as a trafficking hotspot because of the rituals that are centred around the Thimmalapura temple, which is in Bellary on the Andhra Pradesh–Karnataka border. The information I had was that the descendants of devadasis worked as prostitutes here, as in other places. I had been in touch with an NGO which looked into the rehabilitation of sex workers. The NGO ran an informal school in the village of Halliya, just before Kudligi, which was our first destination. Bhaskara, who founded the NGO in 1994, gave us a warm welcome. Bhaskara told us that all the 20 children studying in the organization at the time were the children of devadasis.

He claimed that the devadasis who had turned to prostitution had been persuaded to other avenues of employment and that their children were now the NGO's responsibility. He then introduced us to Gauri, a teacher who was also the daughter of a devadasi. Her mother had turned to prostitution to ensure an education for her. When Gauri attained puberty, several people advised that she too be turned into a devadasi. Her mother agreed. But Gauri was determined to study, and she completed her education till pre-degree, which enabled her to teach at the school now. Unlike in Davanagere, the struggle against the devadasi system had not been very successful here. Mothers continued to be willing to give up their daughters as devadasis as they still did not have any better means of sustenance. I assumed that only a few people had benefited from the organization's activities.

As we travelled to Thimmalapura, Bhaskara hurriedly made a few calls. On arriving at Thimmalapura, almost a hundred women welcomed us. Bhaskara said they were all rehabilitated sex workers. A well-dressed woman then came forward and spoke to Bhaskara in undertones. Bhaskara gave her some instructions, which she repeated aloud to the other women. Immediately, some chairs were brought forth, and the women sat down in front of them. Bhaskara asked us to sit on the chairs, and as soon as we did, a young girl came up and began singing a song in praise of Basaveswara.

The arrangements seemed like everything had been pre-planned. The song was a plea to Sree Basaveswara for the prosperity of the village. As soon as it got over, Bhaskara introduced us to the women. When he announced we were there to study their lives, some smiled artificially.

Most, however, were indifferent.

Vijayamma, a woman in her fifties, then got up and started talking about her experiences. She said she came from a scheduled caste community and was turned into a devadasi during her childhood. Her mother and grandmother were devadasis too, so there had been no other option for her. Her life had been extremely miserable until the NGO made things better. She said that most women like her had turned to alternate modes of employment but could not continue in those as villagers discriminated against them. The NGO, however, had helped them in every way possible, she asserted. Other women got up to speak after her, and all of them showered praises on the NGO's activities. I thought I was sitting in a public relations event for the NGO. Bhaskara later claimed the NGO had bought cows for them with bank loans and that most women at the event now earned their livelihood by selling the milk.

We realized he would not give us any new information; I comforted the poor women by lying to them that all their problems would soon be solved and decided to move on.

Bhaskara, however, did not let us go. He told us more people were waiting to meet us in a colony named Ujjini. There too a large group of women began to list out their problems. The stories were much the same, and they too sang the praises of the organization. From Ujjini we went to Kudligi, where Bhaskara told us about the NGO's activities once more in the organization's head office. He said he could give us photographs of all their activities in a pen drive. I tried to avoid it and asked him to send it by email. But he insisted on giving a pen drive. He opened his drawer to reveal a huge collection of 4 GB pen drives kept inside. I was stunned. These pen drives had been readied for the exclusive purpose of giving visitors a ready reckoner on their activities. While in Davanagere, preventive action against the devadasi system had not progressed beyond street theatre, Bhaskara had used latest technology to further his work.

We finally bid goodbye to Bhaskara and proceeded to the heart of Kudligi, where we saw middle-aged women standing along with their young daughters, scanning their prospects for the evening. Unlike in other places, women here did not seem to beg for attention. They merely relied on eye contact and their smiles. They did not peddle discounted rates either. In their world, those who required their services should come to them, not the other way around.

Kudligi is not characterized by the small, cramped houses that are typical of many such towns. Most of the houses here are spacious and tastefully painted. When customers approach the women, it is the mothers who do most of the talking, while the daughters stand aside, bound by propriety. The mothers also list out the rates for their daughters. To a mother, all her daughters are the same, but it is not so for a customer. So the mother realizes this, and the rates vary accordingly. While the oldest may charge 3,000 rupees, younger daughters would command 5,000.

Kudligi residents are also adept at stopping the police right at the town's entrance. This seems to be the sole occupation for its male residents. The rates the mothers demand take into account all such expenses. If the customer is not wealthy enough to afford her 'wares', the mother is generally ready to go herself for a lesser rate. By no means will she reduce the rates for her daughters. Perhaps this aura of 'dignity', which has been created by their preconditions and toughness, has scaled up their demand and popularity.

When we asked one of the mothers if there would be enough space inside her house for two people to spend the night, she happily welcomed us inside saying we could dine and sleep there and that we did not have to wait till nightfall. We assured her we would return at night and quietly left.

In *Ravindrante Yathrakal* (Ravindran's Travels) by the Malayalam author Ravindran, I had read about the 'urban brides' of Rajahmundry in Andhra Pradesh who would fulfil the desires of the travellers who visited the town. Why had I never heard of the 'brides' of Kudligi before?

The evening grew dark quickly. As we approached NH13, which connects Solapur to Bengaluru, we could see women on either side of the road entice the long-distance lorry drivers. Some of them were chosen, some were completely ignored. Yet they continued to wait with renewed hope as the next lorry drove in. As I looked at those weary faces, I was amazed to find some of them were the same women who had been introduced to me earlier in the morning as beneficiaries of rehabilitation!

My initial shock and disbelief gave way to understanding. These women had entered the list of rehabilitated women to fill their stomachs. Their resolve to solicit customers on the highway too served the same purpose.

Similarly, there were several who filled their stomachs through fake rehabilitation records. The voice of the young girl who sang the chants of Basaveswara worship echoed in my mind.

# 5

# Legend and Tradition in Rajahmundry

I MET VENKATA RAO, WHO CAME FROM ANDHRA PRADESH, on the train from Kudligi to Kerala. We initially talked about Naxals in Warangal, but as I was sharing my experiences in Davanagere and Kudligi, Rajahmundry came to my mind. I compared notes with him about the writings of Ravindran that described the town, but Venkata was quick to correct me that the Rajahmundry of yore no longer existed and that the 'urban brides' Ravindran had described in his book had disappeared long ago. But I wanted to verify this for myself and thus decided Rajahmundry would be my next destination. My BSF friend Pramod came along too.

Rajahmundry is the cultural capital of Andhra Pradesh and was once the capital of the Cholas. At that time, it was known as Rajamahendravaram, which got morphed into

Rajahmundry over time. This was also the headquarters of an eponymous district, and due to its large size, it was split into Eastern Godavari and Western Godavari, in 1859. Currently, Rajahmundry falls in Eastern Godavari.

The history that its residents would prefer to tell is that of its central jail, where several freedom fighters were held captive by the British. However, even many years after independence, the town continues to be known for its sex workers, who caught hold of clients in the name of the erstwhile tradition of *bhogamelas* (festival of sensual pleasures).

Till the end of the 1980s, women were facilitating sex trade around most temples in the coastal districts of Andhra Pradesh. Women would perform in wealthy households during times of celebrations, which would be called *bhogamelas*. These performances were characterized by songs laden with sexual innuendos and dance steps that matched the same, creating a sexually charged atmosphere. The women would be appointed by the folks who controlled the temples to dance and sing at the temples and would be known as *kalavanthalus*, meaning 'an aesthete'. Over time, the word grew extremely stigmatized.

Compared to the devadasis in Karnataka, the *kalavanthalus* were closer to the original devadasi tradition. While the jogammas of Karnataka performed routine temple chores, *kalavanthalus* focused on dance and music. Both groups ended up as servants in temples owing to their poverty and ignorance. Though the current generation of *kalavanthalus* would like to believe their ancestors were privileged and protected by the temple, the truth remains that most were being used by priests and the zamindars as concubines. Moreover, whenever wealthy people came on pilgrimages, the *kalavanthalus* would entertain them as required to ensure that the wealth of the men was directed to the temple. Hence, it became imperative for a temple to maintain *kalavanthalus*.

History tells us that when the advent of Buddhism threatened the hold of Hindu temples in Andhra Pradesh, they relied primarily on the *kalavanthalus* to counter the effect. The wealth amassed through the devadasis was used to rein in the devotees. There was also a time when a temple's eminence was measured by how many devadasis it nurtured. When the temples' influence declined and devadasis were banned by law, the women fell into difficult times. That was when *bhogamelas* became popular once again in places like Rajahmundry. Though these performances began as classical dance and music shows, they would soon give way to sexually laden performances. The festival would end with the landlords inviting the women into their chambers.

When these *bhogamelas* were banned by law in 1988, *kalavanthalu* women were forced to shift to outright prostitution. However, unlike regular brothels, their boudoirs were not meant to merely satisfy one's lust and leave. Dance and music had pride of place here. The women opened their chambers to strangers as a way to display their proficiency in the arts. The art of lovemaking was part of it. They took money from their customers as payment for their cultural flair. They saw the act of lovemaking as something their artistic labours naturally culminated in. They genuinely believed it was wrong to keep their talent hidden from connoisseurs. That was how Rajahmundry and its surrounding areas became a hotbed of pleasure houses in the first half of the twentieth century.

In Rajahmundry, the Godavari spread as far as the eye could see. The railway bridge stretched across to the other bank and evoked curiosity and fear at the same time. Below the bridge was Rajahmundry's famous Gautami Godavari navigation port, and right next to this was the Isuka Veedhi, the erstwhile famed commercial centre when the British held Rajahmundry as headquarters of Godavari district.

Today, for those who are led here by reading its history, Isuka Veedhi is disappointing. Though the buildings have the same antiquated look, no mesmerizing signs of its past glory are visible. After we traversed its lanes, we began to wonder if we had lost our way. We finally stopped by at a house whose board read 'Adv. R Sasikala'.

Sasikala was a 32-year-old sprightly woman who told us how Isuka Veedhi changed its name and form. 'The street used to have brahmins on one side and *kalavanthalus* on the other. The *kalavanthalus* were nothing short of prostitutes, and people solicited their services from all over at all times of the day. The flow of strangers day and night gave rise to security issues. Besides, the frequent brawls between these women and their clients ruined the peace and quiet of the neighbourhood. Moreover, it was giving the locality an unsavoury reputation. This became untenable, and the younger people in town then decided to take a stand against this.

'Thereafter, whenever strangers arrived in any of the homes, the younger people would swing into action and inform the police. Once the police started tightening the ropes and implementing the law strictly, most of the women were forced to withdraw from prostitution. Those who insisted on sticking to the profession were forced to vacate the place.'

Sasikala claimed that they had totally eradicated prostitution in Isuka Veedhi over the past 10 years. She proudly informed us that she herself had called the police on several occasions. However, despite removing the *kalavanthalus*, the street name continued to evoke them. Residents then decided to rename it as Water Works Street, since this was from where water was pumped to various spots in Rajahmundry. In the town's land records, however, it is referred to as Netaji Subhash Chandra Bose Road.

I asked Sasikala why they had not tried to retain and protect the community that had epitomized the indigenous dance and music of Rajahmundry while helping to wean them off prostitution. She smiled and said, 'There was no music and art; it was just plain prostitution.'

Peddapuram is an hour-long bus ride from Rajahmundry. Several families from the bhoga community that once made a living from music and dance have lived here for long. Families evicted from Isuka Veedhi have taken refuge in Peddapuram, which can no longer be termed a village. Though it is dotted with several old temples and cycle-rickshaws, Peddapuram has begun to show the signs of turning into a city.

I couldn't find anybody who could tell me more about the *kalavanthalus*, probably because I could understand most south Indian languages except Telugu. Even when I found someone, they tried to avoid the topic by saying that the tradition of *kalavanthalus* and their pleasure houses were a thing of the past. One man told me the tradition had originated from two temples in the area and that the women who were brought in to dance at these temples later became prostitutes. According to him, there were more than a hundred such families here until recently, but most of them had moved out when the police tightened their hold. However, we did get hints that those who wanted their services would not turn away disappointed. As per his instructions, we started walking from Peddapuram centre to Dargapet. But in Dargapet, most of the houses were shut, and though we passed 10–15 homes, no one followed us or called out to us. Things were not the same as in Ravindran's book. Either prostitution was not practised here any longer or the police had kept a strict check on sex workers.

I had hoped to meet the *kalavanthalus* and understand their situation first-hand, but I was disappointed that my efforts were bearing no fruit. Despite walking up and down the town centre many times, not a single agent approached me. Then, someone wearing a lawyer's coat walked towards us. He introduced himself as Jonathan Rao and pointed us to another lane we hadn't noticed. He told us that the descendants of *kalavanthalus* now lived in that area. He advised us to meet with a lady named Aishah who was working to rehabilitate the community. Before leaving, he warned us that soliciting pleasure houses without informing the police could result in raids.

Right at the beginning of the lane, a man jumped out of a parked auto and came to us. One of his legs had a bandaged wound and seemed to be affected by elephantiasis. He told us in Telugu that young girls were available at cheap rates. Though we understood what he said through his gestures, we began to worry how we would communicate further as we followed him into a narrow lane just wide enough for one person.

A few houses later, three or four girls hurriedly got up and stood in a doorway when they saw us and welcomed us cordially in Hindi. We were relieved and curious at the same time. How did these girls who had never stepped out of Peddapuram learn Hindi?

Before we could ask them, another voice called us from inside in Hindi, 'Come in, sir.'

I asked her, 'Do you know Hindi?'

The woman laughed flirtatiously, opening her paan-filled mouth. 'Arre, first come in, sir.' Though she wore a *davani*, a south Indian two-piece sari, she didn't look like she was from the region.

There were four women inside that house, who immediately reminded me of the sex workers awaiting clients in metropolises. With their fair skin and voluptuous bodies, none of them looked like they were a Peddapuram native. One who looked the oldest gestured to us to sit at her bedside.

As we did so, she asked us point-blank, annihilating in a flash all the legends of courteousness and artistic excellence attributed to Peddapuram, 'How long do you want? Half an hour or one hour?' The pleasure houses of Peddapuram were once famed for their decorated walls, but here there was nothing on the walls other than faded limescale. The woman repeated her question, this time a trifle more roughly. 'How many hours, sir?'

'What's the rate?' I asked, just as a customer would.

'Two thousand rupees for one hour,' she replied, raising two fingers to make her point clear.

'Isn't that too much?' I haggled like a regular.

'How is that too much?' she retorted. It was obvious she was displeased with my attitude.

'The other places I have been to don't charge as much,' I provoked her with my fake bravado.

'What places?' she asked disdainfully. 'We have also been there.'

'Where?' I asked defiantly.

'Have you heard about Kamathipura in Mumbai? We were there for a long time. When the place became too crowded to guarantee a good business, we moved here.'

'So you aren't a native?' I enquired anxiously.

'No,' she said brusquely.

'Who brought you here?' I wanted to get a clearer picture.

'All you need to know is that there are people who do that. Do you agree to 2,000 per hour? Or half an hour?' she persisted, making it clear she would not entertain any further questions.

'Let me check in other places. If the rate doesn't work out, I will come back here.' I slowly got up to leave.

My hostesses didn't like it one bit. 'Are you here to note down official rates?' one of them asked gruffly.

I left without a response.

There was no abuse or attack against a customer like me who left without giving them any business, unlike in other markets. Maybe they knew that if they dealt unpleasantly with the few clients they received, they wouldn't get any new ones. And as soon as we emerged from the house, a young man approached us professionally and gestured he had much better 'items'. I asked him if they knew Hindi. Our guide assured us they did.

When we said we wanted to meet Aishah, he said there was no such person here. He insisted we should check out the girls he had. We managed to avoid him saying we would come back later and continued to look for Aishah.

As we walked down the road that Jonathan had pointed, we came upon a concrete house that was bigger than the others in the neighbourhood and had a picture of Jesus Christ on the wall. With an Arabic name like Aishah, I doubted this would be her home. But a passer-by confirmed this was indeed Aishah's house.

Aishah answered the door wearing a nightdress, her face drowsy from an interrupted sleep. She invited us to come inside. From the interiors, one could make out it had not been long since she had converted. The word 'Om' was still visible on the threshold, and there were pictures of Hindu gods on the walls. The house seemed to be well-furnished with modern amenities. We told her that we had come to talk about *kalavanthalus*. Aishah seemed not only uninterested but also afraid. But then she opened up slowly.

She told us that Vakkalingavara, the street, was once exclusively occupied by *kalavanthalus* but now Muslim, Christian and Hindu girls all worked here. Most of the *kalavanthalu* women were into prostitution, according to her. She told us she had been able to free several of them from sex work through her work. Jonathan had also arrived, and he acted as our translator. He praised her a great deal, saying she had helped women start businesses of their own. There was also funding coming in from abroad, Jonathan enthusiastically added.

Aishah was rather worried by now. She managed a feeble smile and asked us if our conversation would get printed in the papers. She wasn't too convinced when we said no, and refused to speak further. We then left Aishah and Jonathan to their discussions.

On our way back, I noticed that the front yard of several homes had *kolams* in the shape of a cross. Several verandas had the pictures of Hanuman and Jesus Christ sharing the same space. Though they seemed to present a novel example of secularism, I was troubled by the thought that this was not the reality.

What was clear was that several vested interests had come together to exploit the good repute earned by *kalavanthalus* through their dedication to dance and music and had instead turned Peddapuram into a flesh market, an alternative for sex workers who could not flourish in other places. What a change of fortunes for the Peddapuram of yore! Once, the *bhogamelas* gave sleepless nights to many families. Today, the silence of the night was disrupted by the haggling of clients. Then there were the hymns of those for whom the prohibition against sex work had become an opportunity to introduce the women to new gods and enabled them to bring in foreign money. I realized that I needed to travel more to find the original devadasis, the ones who are said to have been a privileged and revered lot. My next destination was Draksharamam, an hour away from Peddapuram, where several *kalavanthalus* were said to reside. Draksharamam today is a rather largish village that doesn't have the crowds and superficial progress of Peddapuram. Upon arriving, we headed to the RCM church, where the priest Father Srinivas introduced us to two nuns. Both insisted they had not heard about *bhogamelas* or the devadasi system being active in the village since they arrived. They said they studied the social issues of a place whenever they were posted there, and if there were reports of something like this, they would surely know about it. They then made several calls, and finally as a last resort, they took us to a priest named Father Ashish Jolly.

Ashish Jolly told us the devadasi system had been well-established around the Bheemeswara temple in the village. 'Once the practice was banned, these women had to turn to prostitution. Christian missionaries then stepped in to help them. Most *kalavanthalus* here were saved from starvation because of the missionaries that have brought about huge changes here,' he extolled. The Bheemeswara temple is the epicentre of Draksharamam, whose history is intricately linked to that of the temple. In earlier times, many of the bhoga families lived here under the temple's protection. Later they moved to other parts of Draksharamam, and brothels opened up in all those places. Till the 1980s, these had a strong influence. Today, however, Draksharamam seems to be in a hurry to cover up this disgraceful past.

Several saffron-clad people outside the Bheemeswara temple acquainted us newcomers with the temple's rituals and practices. But when we asked them about *kalavanthalus,* they were not willing to speak. They knew no language except Telugu, fortifying our belief that no non-Andhra persons visited the temple usually. We finally came upon one person who spoke English. Amidst enquiries about the temple, I slipped in a query about *kalavanthalus*. He said all of them were now camped at a nearby village called Yellavaram and hastily added they had nothing to do with the temple now.

It was evident that prostitution was being practised in Yellavaram. Unlike their tradition, there was no dignified reception of guests here. Rather, women had been reduced to ordinary sex workers like in many other places. On our way back to Draksharamam, we serendipitously met with Jegathiswaran, a percussion artiste who once accompanied *bhogamela* performers. After we explained our motives and he could ascertain we were not from the police, he grew comfortable enough to open up. He confirmed that *bhogamelas* had ended in Draksharamam 20 years ago, in the 1990s.

'I used to coordinate the musicians and dancers and attend such functions. *Bhogamelas* would be highly solicited at special functions such as marriages, and wealthy landlords would approach us for a performance. The pay was excellent. We would get 1,000–2,000 rupees per day, which was a big sum in those days. If the dancers were good, we would get more. And when wealthy landlords wanted to show off, they would call for the best dancers regardless of the expense. Whether or not such performances ended in the landlord's private chambers was up to the dancer.' He reiterated, however, that he had not conducted any such events after the ban.

He told us about a tradition called *kannerakam* conducted among bhoga communities. As per the practice, as soon as a girl from their families attained puberty, the wealthy landlords would bid to deflower her. The girl would then be auctioned off to the highest bidder. Jegathiswaran said he knew many girls who had received thousands of rupees through the practice. He also hinted that several girls who had been bought by the landlords in auction were then taken to Kolkata and sold there once the landlords had enough of them. He tried hard to remember the name of the place in Kolkata; we immediately realized he was talking about Sonagachi.

Relegating his glorious past to his stories, Jegathiswaran was now content to live out an uneventful life as a shopkeeper selling chemical fertilizers. Though he hadn't forgotten the past, he could not ignore the present-day situation of bans either. But what of the women? We tried to look for answers on the streets of Draksharamam and found that several former sex workers had been forced into other jobs, while some even had to leave the village.

We left for Ramachandrapuram, just six kilometres away, where brightly painted buildings that were either churches or prayer halls greeted us. Standing tall with crosses at the top, these were the new refuges for people who were deprived of their livelihoods and on the verge of starvation. The roadside was adorned with flex boards and banners that sported pictures of Jesus Christ along with some new gods. Many houses had nameplates with hilarious combinations of ancient Telugu names with typical Christian names, such as Selvan George and Lakshmana John.

I couldn't help but feel that although the devadasi tradition in Karnataka was different from the *kalavanthalu* system in Andhra, in both places religion was being peddled to those who were suffering. My investigation was not along those lines, however. I now wanted to enquire about the scores of girls packed off to Sonagachi by the landlords. The *kalavanthalus* who had moved out of Draksharamam, Peddapuram and other districts of Andhra Pradesh had also moved to Sonagachi. What stories would Sonagachi have in store?

# 6

# A Life Meant to Serve

THE DEVADASI TRADITION WAS ONCE DEEP-ROOTED IN PURI, Odisha, too. Though the stories I had heard about devadasis at the Puri Jagannath temple seemed exaggerated, I could not dismiss them entirely because of what I had learnt in Karnataka and Andhra Pradesh.

Puri is on the eastern coast of India, 60 kilometres from Bhubaneswar. Among the four holiest Hindu pilgrimage sites that are known as the 'Char Dham' (the four abodes) – the other three being Rameswaram, Badrinath and Dwarka – the city's cultural history is closely entwined with the history of the Jagannath temple.

An autorickshaw took us down a narrow, dirty lane that could hardly accommodate two people at the same time. On one side, water stagnated in a dirty drain, while on the other, decrepit two-storeyed buildings stood cramped against each other. Flies were omnipresent. They sat on the snacks available at the roadside stalls and hovered over the open sores of cows and dogs.

This narrow lane opened out into a wide area that was the main entrance to the Jagannath temple. Beggars jostled for prime space here. One man lay on the ground, unable to move, his body besieged by flies. Those who were waiting in queue for the *darshan* were troubled by the flies too. And as troublesome as the flies were, so were the *karmi*s (ritual priests) who scavenged outside the temple. They would surround anyone who arrived there and offer to perform all the pujas for a meagre *dakshina* (payment in lieu of religious services) of a thousand rupees. If a customer was an experienced haggler, this amount could be brought down to as less as a hundred rupees.

We found that the *karmi*s retreated immediately when we told them we were there to meet the devadasis who once served Lord Jagannath. We asked a rickshaw puller, who assumed we were asking about dance, so he took us to a dance school. Luckily, the man at the dance school understood us better and gave the rickshaw puller the correct directions before seeing us off.

We were taken to Dolamandap Street, which lies adjacent to the temple. The rickshaw halted in front of a dingy passageway. The rickshaw puller stepped down and repeatedly called out, 'Babu...' Finally, a bare-chested man ran down and introduced himself as Achintya Sharma. Since he only knew Odia, the only thing he seemed to pick up from our explanations as to why we were there was the word 'devadasi'. He then invited us to join him through gestures. We followed him up the stairs. It was pitch dark, and our host apologetically explained that power would only be restored by 5 p.m. It was 2 p.m. at that point.

The stairway opened up into a cramped room, which also lay in darkness. A woman loudly asked for something, but no one responded to her. Achintya asked us to sit inside. As our eyes adjusted to the darkness, things slowly started taking shape. Clothes were piled up in whatever available space there was in the room. Suddenly, we realized an emaciated woman lay on a mat on the floor, clumsily wrapped up in an old sari. Despite the darkness, we could make out the wrinkled skin on her hands and feet and on her face too. She groaned and whined, sometimes loudly. Achintya told us her name was Prakruti, she was nearly deaf, and that she had danced before Lord Jagannath at the temple till the day the ban on the devadasi system was implemented in the state. She was the last of the Odia devadasis.

When we told her we wanted to know about her life as a devadasi, she forgot about all her infirmities and requested Achintya to help her sit up. The effort involved in merely sitting up seemed to wear her out. Her breathing became more laboured, and the groans became louder. I grew frightened to see her strain like that. She began to talk slowly. Though deaf, she cupped her ears and caught a few portions of our questions.

'Is your name Prakruti?' I asked loudly.

'Prakruti devadasi,' she corrected me, pride evident in the way she uttered the word 'devadasi'. Achintya got his school-going son Ajay to help us with the translation. Ajay, who was not yet 15, could hardly manage himself, with only a smattering of Hindi he had picked up at school. But he managed to translate our queries into Odia and Prakruti's answers into Hindi for us.

Prakruti was made a devadasi at the tender age of 7 after her family had promised to make their daughter one. She was now 85. 'Certain brahmin families traditionally offered their children as devadasis,' she explained. 'I was from one such family. I was privileged to be a servant of Lord Jagannath. We were trained in dance and music at the temple. I learnt everything from experts. Why do girls study music and dance? To please their husbands. We devadasis too learnt the arts to please our husband – none other than Lord Jagannath. I have pleased him with my skills – from the age of 7 to 79.' Her treasure chest of memories opened up, unfazed by the passage of time.

When the devadasi dance was banned in Puri in 2005, Prakruti was 79. The doors to the sanctum sanctorum would close at 10 p.m., and the traditional belief was that its lord should drift off to sleep after being delighted by the sight of the beautiful women who were dancing for him. For decades, Prakruti said, the lord had been lulled to sleep by her dance, her eyes glistening with pride at the memory. 'Jagannath would only sleep if the dance and the music was up to the mark. We could not compromise on them.'

Prakruti spoke just as a dedicated wife would talk about her husband's likes and dislikes. She believed that her dance was perfect because of the virtuous deeds she had accrued from previous births and that those blessings would last her for several lifetimes. One has to follow the conduct of a faithful wife to receive such blessings, she explained. Devadasis had to be absolutely chaste and true to their husband. She reminded us that her only bridegroom was the lord. She had adopted Achintya as her son, a decision that was taken with the permission of the lord. 'As I lived according to the conditions laid down for a devadasi, the lord gave me good fortune,' she said.

Good fortune! I recoiled at the thought. Did she think her current condition – huddling on a tattered mat on the floor with all her aches and pains in a dark room – was a marker of good fortune? I didn't want to interrupt her, so I didn't say anything. She continued to dig out the memories.

Prakruti recollected there were around 50 devadasis during her heyday, all of whom had taken the vow of chastity and remained true to the lord till the end. All of them had fallen to the vagaries of age. Only she remained. She told us that until 2005, the devadasi dance was conducted as a ritual at the closing time of the Jagannath temple. In later days, this duty fell entirely upon Prakruti. When Achintya remarked that she danced gracefully and unruffled by the frailties of her old age, Prakruti demurely said it was her duty as a wife to put her husband to sleep. 'When the lord himself lies down before you to see your dance, how can you not give your best?' she asked. As she recounted her past, Prakruti began to sing without anyone's prompting. The songs did not express just devotion but a deep love for Jagannath. One line went, 'I am so lucky to be your servant. Wake up soon for me to put you to sleep again at night.'

There was no quiver in her voice as she recollected the songs, no loss of memory. She synchronized her mudras to the song as much as she could while seated on her mat. I thought that if she could stand, she would forget all her infirmities and dance once more in ecstasy. I wanted to click a picture of her singing, and Ajay brought an emergency lamp and held it against her face. I wondered if the bright LED lights would bother her. Achintya reassured us, 'Sir, no problem. She is blind. Don't worry. You can take the pictures.'

As the light shone on her face, I was numbed by the vast emptiness in her eyes that had glimmered with the *navarasa* for over seven decades. It was as though the lord had taken away his beloved bride's eyesight because he couldn't bear her looking at others. As we clicked pictures, Prakruti continued to sing. Finally, when it was time for us to leave, I picked out whatever money I had in my wallet and gave it to her. When she realized I had given her money, she blessed us. As she put her hands on our heads, her eyes began to water. Once again she sang glories to her lord, that it was by his grace that people had come from far away to meet her.

Achintya, however, had a different story. According to him, despite dedicating her life to the temple, the the authorities had not provided anything for her. When she was bedridden after an accident with a vehicle, they gave her a few thousand rupees, although the treatment had cost much more. Prakruti interrupted him, however, and did not allow him to continue with his complaints. She went back to reminiscing about her glorious days. Somewhere inside, I thought the loss of her eyesight and hearing was actually a kindness to someone like her who preferred to live in the glory of her past. We bid her goodbye and walked down the narrow stairway. Our mission now was to meet Prakruti's beloved.

The crowd outside the Jagannath temple was unbearable post sunset. No more *karmi*s approached us now, as they had found several clients in the crowd. We followed the sound of bhajans to arrive at a troupe, who seemed to desire an audience as well, going by their gestures. The bhajans lasted as long as the crowds continued to flow into the temple. Once the crowd died out, they toned down their performance and wound up. We finally approached them and asked about the devadasis. They gave us evasive answers, saying those were matters of the past and no longer relevant. The temple doors now closed without the dance of devadasis. Lord Jagannath went off to sleep without anybody to lull him. Slowly, we also took our leave.

One question, however, continued to recur in my mind. How were the devadasis in Puri spared from prostitution unlike in Karnataka? Or was it that we did not happen to see such devadasis?

The fact remained that the devadasi tradition in Puri was absolutely different from that in Andhra and Karnataka. In Andhra and Karnataka, devadasis were chosen from backward castes, whereas in Puri, they came from the upper-class brahmin community. Since they received societal acceptance, several stayed on in the temple after the ban. The strong financial clout of the temple may have shielded them from turning to prostitution. However, had they been denied acceptance from the society at large, it would have been unlikely for them to have perpetually remained as the chaste wives of Lord Jagannath.

I asked around to learn why devadasis were not drawn from the lower castes in Puri. Raj Pandey, a social activist who worked for the upliftment of backward communities in Odisha, gave me an explanation that was logical enough.

'In Odisha, where people belonging to lower castes are not even considered as human beings, the upper-caste brahmin community would not let them into the temple by any means. Even today, there are many temples in Odisha that forbid Dalits from entering, challenging the judiciary system.' According to social activist Jagabandhu Jain, whenever there was shortage of women willing to become devadasis in Puri, men dressed up as women and became devadasis. This seemed to affirm Raj Pandey's views. In Kerala too, devadasis were selected only from the higher castes, as TKD Muzhappilangad writes in his book *Devadasis*. I wondered why higher castes in Kerala and Odisha developed the same outlook while they had a wholly different approach in states like Karnataka.

Several tourist buses were parked near the beachside hotel where we stayed, along with tour operators who offered package tours combining various shrines in one go. We boarded a bus that would show us five major temples for 180 rupees, the chief attraction being the famous Konark Sun Temple. At one point on the bus, the guide pointed to the Parasurameswara temple and announced on the mike, 'This does not belong to us Hindus. This is the temple of the SCs and STs.' No one on the bus was surprised; I realized that people from the lower castes weren't considered Hindus here. I was now convinced that the upper castes here would not allow them to be associated with temples even as devadasis, just as Raj Pandey had suggested.

The Sun Temple bore clear evidence of the devadasi tradition that existed here in the bygone days. A vast *mandap* (dais) once used for dance performances is the main attraction here. A huge stone wheel resembling a chariot wheel is called the 'wheel of life', and each of its spokes depicts devadasis on them. The guide told us that the wheel showed the daily life of a devadasi from morning till evening.

It was now past 5.30 p.m. The setting sun covered its temple with the effulgence of its waning rays. Leaving behind the mesmerizingly beautiful devadasis carved in stone, we continued on our quest to meet real-life devadasis.

# 7

# Sonagachi

AMONG INDIAN CITIES, KOLKATA IS THE OLD LADY WITH grace. The beauty of this city lies in its antiquity. Once the capital of India under the British, its history goes back to the Bhakti movement, which was deep-rooted here. Its modern name is a corruption of 'Kali Ghat'. Here the sun rises earlier than in down south, while city traffic only picks up after 10 a.m. The only ones, however, who make most of the morning are the women of Sonagachi. They line up outside their doors at any time of the day.

History says that in older times, Sonagachi was where the zamindars of Bengal would bring their favourite danseuses and put them up so that they could visit them at will, watch their dance during the day, and wallow in lust at night. A prominent Kolkata historian, P. Thankappan Nair, writes that zamindars flaunted their grandeur by bringing in danseuses from as far as Lucknow and from other villages in Bengal. Being brought to Sonagachi was the ultimate testimony to the proficiency of a danseuse. But there is a world of difference between the old times and modern-day Sonagachi, and to understand why, one needs to saunter around the alleys of Sonagachi several times over.

The alleys and lanes leading to Sonagachi are taken over by the women by 9 a.m. They cast furtive glances at all who pass by. If someone happens to return their glance, they invite them in with another round of eye contact. Some of them draw the attention of the reticent ones with subtle sounds. Most wear jeans and tight T-shirts. Women above 30 seem to wear saris.

At a stall just outside Sonagachi, we drank tea served in small earthen pots. As we sipped on, we assessed the place. Groups of women hung around here and there. Every stranger kindled new hopes in them. As we finished our tea and walked ahead, the catcalls and gestures became louder and more forceful. The women tried various tactics like fiddling with their hair and saris to seduce any prospective clients. Some women sat on their doorsteps and applied lipstick. A group of girls who seemed to be from the North-East gathered outside one of the rooms. All of them knew Hindi and Bengali.

The slightly wider lanes had small shops on either side. Some women sat without any make-up by a meat stall, dressed in their nightwear. I guessed they were the ones who had worked till late.

They passed comments laden with sexual innuendos at the women who were dressed up. Men stood by the tea stalls and in their casual uniforms resembled the villains of popular cinema. Someone called out 'Saab!' from behind us. We turned around to see a man with a big tilak on his forehead approach us. His pot belly was so big that it impaired his gait.

'What age group are you looking for, Saab?' He asked.

We said we did not want any and continued to walk ahead briskly. Though he did try calling us again, he did not pursue us closely after that. A little further, a shirtless old man sat inside a parked rickshaw with a small plastic box next to him, seemingly jobless yet eagerly monitoring everyone who passed by with his eyes in the hopes of finding a client. His body language was typical of that of a pimp. He looked up at us, and his expression told us he wanted to know why we were there. We told him that we were there to learn about Sonagachi. He did not seem to believe us and discouraged our queries. But when we handed him a hundred rupee note, he softened his stance and began to open up.

His name was Sanjay Das, and he was 68. He was born in rural Bengal, far from the city, and poverty brought him to Kolkata. At first, he washed the dishes at a tea shop. Sonagachi had a lot of women in those days too. So he became an agent, linking customers with the girls of their choice. When this fetched him a decent income, he quit his job and became a full-time pimp, now earning around 30,000 rupees per month.

'Thirty thousand?' I asked incredulously.

He pointed at a building across from us and said, 'The monthly rent of that building is ₹1,50,000.' The six-storeyed building looked ancient with its peeling walls and windows without bars. Clotheslines had been pulled across the rooms and had women's clothes drying all over them. One could see years of paan stains below the windows. I did not believe Sanjay Das, so he explained, 'These buildings are all owned by wealthy folks who rent them out to the agents here. The agent who offers the highest rent bags the contract, and only the agent with the best women can afford such high rents. Sometimes they even buy off the building after paying a lump sum. The building that you see in front of us is run by three girls. The one next to it is rented out for 60,000 and has four young girls. If there are younger girls, things are simpler. No amount of commission is too high. And thanks to the beneficence of Kali, there are plenty of young girls who keep coming to Sonagachi.'

'How do we get a young girl?' I asked.

'You have to have money. That's all.' He laughed.

'We are ready. We just want to talk to the girl, that's all,' I said.

'To talk?' He burst out laughing. 'That's not possible. Items are available from 100 rupees onwards. I can arrange them for you. There are smart girls who dance very well and will charge only 1,500 per hour.'

'Is the rate higher for a longer period?'

'2,500 for two hours, 3,500 for three hours, and so on.'

'We want to watch her dance for an hour,' I said.

'You can do whatever you want. That is up to you.'

We paid him 1,500 rupees, and then he told us only one person was allowed inside. When we insisted we wanted to go together, he suggested we take two girls. Finally, we convinced him that we would only watch the dance and went in together.

The building that Sanjay Das took us to was absolutely ancient. As we climbed the stairs to each floor, we could see girls huddled up in their rooms through the windows. Six to seven girls sat on a bed. Hearing us approach, some of them looked us over carefully. The third floor opened up into a huge hall. A thin man was stretched out on a mattress. A girl lay next to him. Another slept on a mat on the floor. Both the girls jumped up upon seeing us. The man on the floor merely turned around and smiled knowingly at Sanjay Das, who then explained our request to the man in Bengali. The man asked for 1,700. We stood our ground and said we only had 1,500. After a lot of haggling, he settled for an extra 50. When we handed over the money to Sanjay Das, he reacted as if he had seen something repulsive and gestured towards the man on the mat. He took the money from us and put it under his pillow. We could see more cash there. 'Which of these do you want?' he asked, pointing to the two girls.

We looked at each other. 'Either is fine,' we said.

However, he seemed to be particular about playing the perfect businessman and insisted we choose one.

Both the girls looked under 18. One wore T-shirt and trousers. The other wore a miniskirt. She wore lipstick even as she slept on the mat. We chose the girl wearing the trousers, and as we did so, the other girl dropped the facade of reverence she had held till then and went back to sleep in relief.

The girl led us up a narrow stairway. Each floor seemed to have seven or eight rooms. Some doors were closed, while we could hear the sound of girls chatting and laughing about from the open ones. When we reached the sixth floor, the girl opened the first room and went inside. As we followed her, my head hit the door ledge. 'The tall guy wasn't careful, eh?' She laughed coquettishly.

She then asked us to sit. We pulled up a stool for her and made ourselves comfortable. 'Do you want to eat anything before the dance?' I asked her.

'Do you want something?' She threw the question back at us.

'We will buy beer if you will have it too,' we said.

'You'll get everything here,' she said. She went out and returned with a middle-aged woman, whom she introduced as their ayah. The woman greeted us, took the money for beers, and left.

Our girl moved to a corner. Draping herself with a sheet, she changed her clothes. She removed her T-shirt and wore a tiny garment that covered only her chest, like a thin cotton bra. Then she removed her pants too.

'Shall we start the dance?' she asked.

'Wait,' we said. 'We have an hour. Let the beer come. Then we will have the dance.' We made her sit on the stool and asked her to tell us her story.

The girl's name was Diya. Though she said she was 19, we were not convinced. While talking, she got up and switched on the CD player and played some Hindi songs. When a particular song played, she turned to us and smiled as if to ask, 'Is this what you want?' We smiled in agreement. She then threw the remote on the sofa and sat on the stool again.

When the ayah brought us the beers, Diya threw off the sheet before answering the door in her underwear. She covered herself again when she sat back on the stool. When she went out to buy paan, she threw off her sheet once more. I realized this was for others to think she was dancing inside the room. She raised the volume of the CD player so that our conversation could not be heard outside. We spoke loudly to be heard above the music, but her voice remained at the same level. She gave us a fairly good description of Sonagachi and its way of life. But when it came to her personal life, Diya was wary.

When the beer got to her head, she started speaking very fast. When we repeated certain questions, she asked if we were from the police. We immediately said no. When her words started muddling up, we asked her about her family once more. By now, either she didn't doubt us or maybe she just didn't care, but Diya opened up finally. 'It's been 18 months since I came to Sonagachi. I come from a small village in Maharashtra. My parents are farmers. I have two sisters too.

'Agriculture is not something you can depend on. Since it almost never gives the expected yield, we starved most of the time. Then one day, an agent came home and told my father he would take my sister to Kolkata. He gave my father 10,000 rupees to bring my sister here. That was an unthinkable sum for my parents. Moreover, they were relieved on multiple counts – that my sister would not have to starve any more and they only had two more daughters to worry about. When the harvest disappointed us again, it was my turn. Maybe my parents thought I too would live a life without starvation like my sister. I reached Sonagachi soon after I turned 16 and was brought to a lady everyone called Didi. Life is good here,' she said, 'I at least get food.' Her face, however, implied otherwise. Perhaps she too realized this, so she deliberately avoided looking at our faces and instead insisted on changing the song.

When Diya started chewing paan along with her beer, an unbearable stench filled the room. We expressed our discomfort. She immediately went out and spat the paan like a good host. Back in the room, she drank the beer and continued to talk. 'I serve up to three men in a day. At least two for sure. We never ask them where they come from or what they do. They don't ask us anything either. The money is given to Didi. She is the one who provides us with food and shelter. She buys us pretty dresses too. A beautician comes here to do our make-up. Everything is looked after by Didi.'

'So you won't get any of the money we paid?' I asked.

'Why do I need money here? We get everything we need without paying money,' Diya quipped indifferently.

'Do you want to come with us and see Kolkata?' I asked her as a means to get to know her mind.

'No. They won't let me go,' she replied.

'Do you wish to see Kolkata?' I prodded further.

'No,' she said quietly, lowering her head.

'We know that you want to go out. Why can't you speak truthfully?' we asked.

She was amused, and she laughed and pinched my hand. Taking advantage of that, I pushed again. 'Tell me truthfully. Don't you wish to see Kolkata?'

She looked at me without saying a word, and I returned her look, expecting her to say something. Finally, she asked, 'Why?'

'Who is your closest friend?' I asked.

'Rani,' she replied enthusiastically to the unexpected question and began telling us about her. Rani was a 22-year-old Bengali girl.

'Didn't you have any friends back home?' I asked her.

She mumbled something, so I moved closer and asked her if she ever wanted to see them. 'No,' she replied softly. It was very obviously a lie.

'Don't you wish to see your parents?' I asked gently.

She did not have the will to lie any more and remained quiet. When I offered her the beer, she reached for it eagerly and finished off the whole bottle. I could sense she now drank only to avoid answering that question.

The CD player continued to play a medley of songs. When the song 'Teri Meri' from the movie *Bodyguard* came on, she started singing along and moved her body rhythmically to the tune.

'Who is your favourite actor?' I asked.

'Shahrukh.'

'Are you allowed to go out to watch movies?'

'No, we watch it on TV here.'

'Can't you go back home and live happily with a husband and children, like they show in the movies?'

'Who will feed me and the children then?' she replied.

I did not know what to say. She pinched my hand flirtatiously again.

'Whatever you say, Diya, this is not the way to live. You

will eventually become unwanted. Your Didi will kick you out. How will you live then? If you were to go home and get married, you will have your husband for company. Your children will take care of you when you grow old. Don't you wish for that secure life?' I asked.

She looked at the floor for the longest time before replying slowly, 'Didi is cruel... we know that. You are good people.'

'Shall we give you some money?' I asked.

'What is the point?' she asked pragmatically. 'I can't do anything with that money.'

I had nothing left to ask, so I checked the time on my phone. It was almost 1 p.m. We had been inside for more than an hour and a half. I could see two missed calls from Urmi Basu, whom I had promised to meet at 12.30 p.m. Urmi was the founder-trustee of the AIDS prevention project. I grew restless and wondered if I had missed my appointment.

Diya noticed my discomfort and asked, 'Is it time to go?'

'Yes.'

She got up. I asked for her number, making a mental note to call her for any information I might have missed. She gave it immediately.

'You should get out from here and lead a happy life,' I advised her again.

She surprised me with her response. 'I want to hug you,' she said. Before I could say anything, she hugged me. She hardly reached till my chest, so I could not make out the emotions on her face. I wondered what was going through her mind.

Suddenly the phone vibrated in my pocket. It was Urmi Basu. I grew worried that she would be offended if I delayed our appointment any further. I thought of how to evade Diya.

'We will come again. You will be here, right?' I asked.

'Definitely,' she said and opened the door. We stepped out behind her.

While walking down, we saw the girls through the windows again. Some checked the clock curiously and expressed their doubts. Some made what seemed like seedy comments to Diya. We could not understand anything. Nor did we ask.

When we walked down two floors, Diya abandoned all familiarity and ran inside the hall without even turning to look at us. The man who took the money waved us goodbye. We did not speak to each other as we descended the three floors. I felt a sense of guilt and self-scorn come over me. While the young sex worker had ingenuously displayed her affection towards me, I had only looked out for my next source with the cold heart of a journalist.

Urmi waited for us at a Café Coffee Day in Ballygunge Circular, 10 kilometres from Sonagachi. She had informed us that she would try to tell us as much as possible in the one hour she had kept aside for us with much difficulty. Urmi, who had done a master's in social work, had been moved by the plight of sex workers and had started her NGO called New Light. Her dream was a day when the sex workers of Sonagachi would be employed elsewhere. Urmi genuinely believed such a day would come. But she was clear about the obstacles too.

'Middlemen control the politics and administration of this place,' she explained, 'and that is the biggest stumbling block.' The CPM had ruled West Bengal for nearly 35 years. 'But they could not rehabilitate a single person. What they wanted was votes and therefore could not displease the middlemen here. We on the other hand stand by the women.'

'Is the rehabilitation of more than 10,000 women feasible?' I sceptically asked her.

'I'll come to that,' she said. 'Many girls here have been lured in on false promises from Nepal and Bangladesh. Once they arrive, the girls have no contact with the outside world. Doesn't the government have a liability to stop them? Had the BSF not been corrupt, they could have easily saved many girls. The middlemen have to cross the river with the girls from Bangladesh. BSF soldiers are ready to look the other way for as little as 50 or 100 rupees. At least those girls would have been saved had they not done so.'

Pramod, my friend who had been posted in Bengal as a former BSF soldier, stayed quiet. I had expected him to defend the accusation, but he got up and began to take pictures.

I asked Urmi, 'Does New Light focus mostly on spreading awareness?'

'Awareness is important. But that alone won't win the war. We need strong legislation that enables rehabilitation. If you look at the situation here, you will see that the powerful CPM is backing the Durbar Mahila Samanwaya Committee, who fight for the rights of sex workers but don't seem to think the practice itself is wrong. Hence, there is no question of rehabilitation for them. The Trinamool Congress is also afraid of losing their votes like any other political party. Mamata Banerjee stays close to Kolkata's biggest red-light area in Kalighat. What has she done for them? She has not lifted a finger!' Urmi burst out in anger.

'What does New Light do?' I steered her away from politics.

'We have special schemes to protect the children of sex workers. There are schools meant for them. We move the minor girls to shelters. We are currently focusing on rescuing the children of sex workers from this hell. And we try to rescue those who have already become sex workers. We tell them about role models like Balraj and Vishwanath who studied at the Kalighat New Light school and then pursued animation to become successful in life,' Urmi stated proudly.

'Why has New Light centred its activities in Kalighat?' I expressed my doubt.

'Among Kolkata's flesh markets, Kalighat deserves the most attention. Thousands of women prostitute themselves in the alleys near the Kali temple. In the beginning of the 20th century, after sati was abolished, sending widows to the Kali temple was a widespread practice. This turned Kalighat into a centre of prostitution. Several families forced the widows to live their lives by the banks of the Ganga in Kalighat, in service of the goddess Kali. Visitors would exploit such women. That is how Kalighat became a red-light area. The history of Sonagachi only begins when these women moved out from there to find new locations. Thus, any rehabilitation activity in Kolkata had to start from Kalighat.'

'Does the practice of abandoning widows here from other districts exist today?' I asked.

'No. Nowadays the widows of Bengal go to Vrindavan in Mathura, where they live in the bhajan ashrams. I don't think their situation is much better.'

We went back to Sonagachi the next day to look for another Diya. The plan was to talk to the first agent who came our way and pose as a customer as we had done previously. Just as we walked down one of the lanes, a group of women leaped down. Two of them grabbed us by our sleeves. 'Come with us. You will get to choose any type you want,' they said.

'We have just come to see the place,' I said as I shook off her grip.

'You will get a chance to see that as well,' one of the older women jeered. She must have been about 50. The other four looked to be around 30, while one thin girl looked about 25.

'You will get girls from 200 rupees onwards,' the older woman, who seemed to be the leader, said.

'No,' I replied.

'One of you can have her,' she said, pointing to the 25-year-old. 'There is one more like her inside. The other can have her.'

The more I tried to remove her hand, the more her grip tightened. 'We haven't come for that,' I now said sternly.

Their tone changed immediately. 'Let us see how you get out of here then,' the woman yelled. The others turned belligerent. The agents and their goondas were all within shouting distance. We were sure we had no escape. Suddenly, a group of four other women arrived and began to argue with the first group. We hoped this would be our chance to escape, but they didn't let loose the grip on our sleeves even during the argument. When the second group left, our hopes left with them. 'Here, they will take you inside,' the group leader said, pointing to two or three of her gang.

The 25-year-old walked in front of us, while the 30-year-old followed us. Two others closed us in from the sides. As we walked through the lanes, some of the women who were waiting for customers looked at us sympathetically. Others seemed to be angry that they had lost out on an opportunity. As we moved aside to give way to some girls who approached us from the other side, the 25-year-old carefully watched us.

The lane ended in front of two narrow buildings, and we grew more scared. We felt like we were walking into the unknown. I looked at Pramod, who told me with the intrinsic courage of a soldier, 'We don't know whether we will come back alive. Nonetheless, stay brave.' We could see an aged woman sitting in the buff and bathing in the narrow passage. Another cleaned fish. Yet another, potatoes. The pathway grew narrower, and three well-built men stood there menacingly. They said something to the women accompanying us, who laughed and said, 'Yes.' The men looked at us threateningly. Terror surged up inside me. Thankfully, they did not follow us.

The lane got darker, and we could see girls looking at us from their windows on both sides. All lanes inside Sonagachi seemed to be identical. We finally reached a house. As soon as we stepped inside, one of the women accompanying us asked, 'Why haven't you removed your sandals? Don't you see this is our house? Don't you see the picture of Kali Devi?' She pointed towards the pictures on the wall.

We stepped outside and removed our footwear. As we stepped inside, the 25-year-old gestured to me to sit on a bed. But an old lady already slept on it, so I asked her, 'Next to her?'

The young woman laughed and said, 'Just sit. I will come to do the job.' Then as an afterthought, she added, 'We don't go back on our word. Kali is our protector.'

I sat next to the old woman. Pramod was put in a room next to mine that was separated by a curtain. One of the women accompanying us slammed the door shut.

'Twelve hundred rupees.' The 25-year-old extended her hand.

'We don't have that much money with us. We just came to see everything,' I said shakily.

'You don't have the money?' she asked me incredulously and then snatched the wallet out of my pocket and counted the money in it. 'Where have you hidden the money?'

'Nowhere,' I replied meekly.

'Stand up!' she ordered.

I complied. She unravelled my rolled-up sleeves and dug deep into all my pockets more thoroughly than the police or the army. When she came upon the voice recorder in my pocket, my heart missed a beat. If she realized what it was, we might not make it out alive.

'What is this?' she asked.

'It's a pen drive. It has all my work-related files. Please don't destroy it,' I beseeched her.

'We don't destroy anything. We are Kali's servants.' She turned to the goddess's picture and chanted a mantra under her breath.

She then went over to Pramod's room and checked his purse. It was empty. She threw the purse on the ground in disgust. 'No money? You've come here without any money? Filthy dog!' she cursed us in Bengali.

'We had just come to see everything,' Pramod repeated the old story.

Her face now flushed with anger, and she let loose a litany of expletives that woke up the old woman. She jumped up and asked me, 'What happened?'

I pretended as if nothing had happened.

By then the woman came back from Pramod's room. 'You don't have enough money for the both of you?' Her anger was barely concealed now.

'The money I had was actually meant for our trip back home,' I said pitifully.

'Where do you have to go?' she asked.

'Madras,' I said.

'Madrasi, don't you have more money?'

'No.'

She then returned the thousand rupees she had taken earlier and told me to go to the room inside. Then she brought Pramod too. We exchanged a few words in our mother tongue. The girl immediately shouted at us, 'How dare you talk to each other in Madrasi?'

The 30-year-old who accompanied us sat in the inside room and asked me to get on the bed, which I did. Then I noticed that the old lady who had been sleeping in the other room now stood behind me. Our interrogator gave her 50 rupees from what she had taken from us. The woman opened her palm and mechanically handed her two condoms. She threw both the condoms at me, said, 'Screw it on,' and left.

The 30-year-old leaned back and rolled up her top in one go. 'Wear the condom quickly,' she said.

'No,' I said.

'It will be dangerous if you don't wear it. Better to wear it.' She now took on the tone of an advisor. She had mistaken my refusal to mean I did not want to wear a condom.

'No, I don't want it. What's your name?' I changed tack immediately.

'Nimi,' she replied, struggling to find a suitable lie in reply to that unexpected question.

'Where do you come from?'

'You do your job.' She urged me, ignoring my questions.

'No.'

'Why?'

'I don't want to,' I raised my voice.

Nimi now started to shout. Within a second, the

'expletives expert' returned, showering profuse expletives once more. Nimi was half naked by now, and the expert tried to remove her pants too. I jumped in to stop her. This enraged her further, and she started to beat me up. Caught between the two, Nimi shrieked in pain and belted out expletives.

'I will do it; you just leave.' I somehow convinced the second woman to leave. Once she had left, I turned to Nimi and helped her pull up her pants, asking her pitifully, 'I just want to go. You got my money, so what's the problem?'

'No, if we take money and don't work, Didi will be angry with us. You do your job,' she urged.

'I will tell Didi you have done it. I just want to leave, please,' I pleaded.

Her mouth slowly curved into a smile, probably because of my pathetic ways. 'Return this guy's money,' she shouted out with a laugh so that those outside could hear her.

Again the interrogator rushed in. 'Look here, you are our first customer today. If you don't do your job, our whole day will be screwed,' she tried to convince us. Nimi was easier to convince, but the interrogator was a pain in every sense.

'We gave you the money. Why is there an issue?'

'Kali will be angry.' She turned the goddess into her ally now.

'Will you please just leave?' I vented my frustration in my mother tongue and pointed a finger at her. She misunderstood me and assumed I was asking for her.

'If you wanted me, you could have just asked.'

She started removing her clothes then and there. I stopped her with a lot of difficulty and sent her off.

Nimi looked at me sympathetically. 'Do you want to leave?' she asked.

I nodded in relief. She got up and adjusted her top properly, sliding her mobile phone back into her bra. She then said something aloud at which our interrogator came in smiling and said generously, 'Go ahead.'

I dashed out. Pramod was already waiting for me. He held my hand to give me courage.

The interrogator then transformed into a calm hostess. 'You should leave this place happy. That's how everyone who comes here leaves. If not, Kali will be angry with us.'

'What if someone else tries to grab us when we leave from here?' I asked.

'No one will touch you. Come with me. I will escort you.' She led us outside with the same passion that she had displayed when abusing us. She walked us out through a different lane. There was no dearth of heartrending scenes here either. An old woman begged for alms. Others ate from rusted bowls.

'Do you think what you did was right?' I collected the courage to ask our interrogator once we were outside the lane.

She didn't reply, and seemed embarrassed.

'What's your name?' I asked.

‘Charu,’ she said and told us about herself as we walked. Maybe she had not wanted us to judge her harshly because of what she had done earlier, so she spoke openly.

‘My home is in Jungle Mahal in Bengal. By home, I mean a few sheets propped up over four bamboo poles. That’s what we call a house in those parts. The stove is placed in a corner, but rarely did we get to light it up. How can we light it if there is nothing to cook? Most times, the stove was a place to pile up coal. We used to roast corn cobs over the coal and eat that. That was our food most of the time. The villagers had no idea of the benefits they were supposed to receive from the panchayat. Let alone that, most people weren’t even getting fair wages. Because of such unbearable exploitation, Maoists slowly got a foothold in our village. My brother joined them two years before I came here. In fact, not just my brother, but all young men of his age had turned Maoists. They took special classes.’

‘Don’t you think the Maoists might have exploited your poverty?’ I prodded to make sure she didn’t lose the thread of her story.

‘I don’t know about all that. We were told that taking up arms was the only way to remove poverty. After my brother and others joined, they began to say that girls should also join the mission. They said for a revolution to happen, boys and girls should fight side by side without any gender discrimination. So, along with a few other girls of my age, I joined the classes a few months after my brother did.

'The Maoists would tell us in class that there would be a better tomorrow. If we did not react, we would starve to death for sure, but if we revolted, at least we had the hope of getting food tomorrow. That made us hopeful. All of us participated in the classes actively. Our parents also did not mind their children becoming Maoists. There was nothing to lose for them, so why fear anything? Moreover, they were ready to send their children anywhere if there was a chance to spare the children from the misery they had gone through.'

'What happened after that, Charu?' I enquired.

'We realized within a year that our hopes for a revolt to liberate us was just wishful thinking. My brother and three of his friends were thrown in lock-up for throwing stones at the police station. When we talked in the classes about attacking the jail and the police station to liberate them, the people who took the classes advised us to be quiet and wait for the right time. That led to disagreements between us. The families of the boys in custody stopped seeing them as friends. Maybe they weren't looking to exploit us. Maybe they were only trying to avoid another crisis and ensure that more people don't get caught and therefore exercised restraint.' Charu did not blame the Maoists for her situation either.

'So, could you bring them out of lock-up?' I couldn't contain my curiosity.

'No,' she replied as a matter-of-fact. 'The Maoists then

lost whatever respect they had earned in the village. The villagers began to feel that an alliance with the Maoists would only ensure jail for them. When the people realized that Maoists could not provide them food or employment, they were no longer willing to send their children to the classes, which gradually stopped. But we still needed a solution for our hunger. So I boarded the train for Kolkata with a few other girls. All our parents knew what the situation here was like.'

Charu didn't know how much her parents were paid for her, but she knew for sure it would have been more profitable than turning her into a Maoist. 'The situation of the villagers might be just as bad today, but at least we girls were saved,' she said with joy.

'Do you think coming here was saving yourself?' I couldn't believe my ears.

'Yes, of course. Which woman has been saved by Maoism?' she retorted.

I remembered her behaviour from earlier. What sort of a Maoist would she have made? We had reached the main road, so I asked her to join us for tea. Notwithstanding the camaraderie with which she had shared her life story till then, she refused. After we had walked ahead for quite a bit, we turned around. Charu continued to stand there, looking at us.

The Durbar Mahila Samanwaya Committee, which fought for the rights of sex workers, was on Nilmoni Mitra Street inside Sonagachi, towards Girish Park metro station. Its president Bharati De had promised to meet us there to give us an overview of her organization and tell us about the rights of sex workers. When we arrived at the reception, the girl behind the desk gave us a knowing smile. We thought we were exchanging pleasantries. Only later did we realize there was more to it. The receptionist made a few calls, smiling meaningfully at us all the while. We were then asked to come back after lunch.

When we arrived again, we found Bharati De engaged in some work at her desk. Her staff led us to her as if we were meeting the CEO of a large business firm. Bharati played good hostess by cutting short the calls that she was receiving continuously on both her mobiles and offered us tea. I decided to cut straight to the chase. 'What is the relevance of the Mahila Durbar in the current scenario?'

'Sex workers have certain rights as workers which need to be protected. That is the relevance of the organization,' she replied automatically.

'Isn't it better to shift them from sex work to some other profession?' I wanted to understand her position.

'What for?' she retorted. 'That would not be practical. There are 12,118 workers here today. What job can you offer them? It is sheer stupidity to expect that a state like Bengal can absorb this large a workforce into any occupation.

Which job will give them the kind of income they make today? If someone does want to take up another job, they are free to do it. But Durbar will not allow them to be forced into another job if they prefer to do this,' she said, making the organization's position clear.

'Isn't there any value for a woman's dignity?' I questioned her further.

'Of course,' she replied readily. 'That is exactly why we fight for the rights of those in this field. It is due to the existence of Sonagachi that women can walk the streets with dignity. Otherwise, crimes like rape would have become common. Our contribution towards maintaining law and order in the country is not negligible. That consideration should also be given to these workers.' Bharati then proceeded to cement her argument with further elaboration. 'When one of us gets "spoilt" in your terms, five ordinary women get to live good lives.' She seemed to be repeating a script fed to her.

'How did you get into this organization?'

'I come from a large family. Poverty was literally killing us, so I was sent off to Sonagachi even before I attained puberty. After coming here, girls like me started getting to eat. That itself was a big deal for most of us. Our biggest problems here are the legal system and the cops who harass us at every possible opportunity in the name of non-existent laws. This made us think about the need to stand united, which resulted in this organization. Moreover, I have also been a CPM worker from my childhood and that also helped in these activities.'

'But despite your party ruling here for 35 years, why did they not do anything to rescue sex workers here?' I asked her.

'You are repeating the same thing. What do you mean by "rescue from here"? Most come here to be rescued from the miseries back home. Do they have better alternatives? What is important is that our rights should be protected while we are here. Our goal is to ensure that the government sees to it. In this matter, the CPM has helped us a lot. In fact, I should say no one has helped us like the CPM has.' Bharati's voice toughened as she said this.

'How do you see the advent of Trinamool in tackling this?' I asked.

'Rehabilitation is not practical, no matter who talks about it. Can anyone rehabilitate us by giving us a job that will give us the same income that we make today?' Bharati challenged.

'But do you support young girls being brought here and locked up in the name of work? Are you in favour of minors working this profession?' I asked bluntly.

'That used to happen long ago. No torture is meted out to any unwilling girl today. If that happens, we move the girls to a shelter and rehabilitate them further. The entry of minors into Sonagachi has been entirely stopped after our organization stepped in. And that is precisely why the group is relevant.'

Bharati's responses seemed orchestrated to these expected questions.

'What else does the organization do?' I asked.

'Earlier, if a girl from Sonagachi got pregnant, that was the end of her career. Today, they can hand over the baby to us without any worries. We make sure the children and their education are taken care of. We support their talents and interests. Children are no more a nightmare for Sonagachi's girls,' Bharati said. 'We have also started a savings scheme like a chit fund wherein an amount is collected from sex workers every day. This amount is rotated to be of use to someone who has an emergency among them. Today, this chit fund has an annual turnover of 25 million rupees. Ninety-five per cent of the people working in this office are sex workers. They have the freedom to go "work" if someone demands sex of them.'

'You say there is nothing wrong in this line of work. Will you allow your children to take this up?'

'If they are interested in it, let them take it up. What's wrong in children taking up the mother's line of work? They should be free to choose whatever profession they want.'

'If someone approaches you, will you go?' I asked, looking into her eyes directly.

Bharati now seemed flustered as she made up some excuses. 'See, I am always in a hurry. I am often travelling abroad. Seminars, discussions, conferences... we want the voice of sex workers to be heard everywhere. I am totally occupied running around for that. Take a look. Both my passports are already exhausted.'

I thought to myself that the people she said she represented would not even know what a passport was. They were simply waiting to fulfil the next set of instructions from her, who they believed would secure the kingdom of heaven for them. What irony!

Bharati arranged for us to speak to other sex workers too – Amrita Das, Ira Ghoshal, Barsha Roy – all of whom told us their stories, which were identical to those of Diya and Charu. The girl at the reception was also a sex worker, who tried to impress upon us how her customers returned to solicit her because of her skills. Only then did I get what her smile in the morning meant.

When both Bharati and other office-bearers were engrossed in various phone calls, I took a calculated risk and approached the sex workers. 'Just because you are getting enough food here now, you imagine this to be a good life. Have you imagined what will happen to you when you are old? Haven't you seen the old women who have been thrown out to fend for themselves? Doesn't the same fate await you too?'

Most of them had an expression that seemed to say, 'What the hell is this fellow talking about?' But one of them seemed to grow pensive. She stood there lost in thought, looking at the floor and running her fingers over her lips. When she saw she was being noticed, she pretended to look elsewhere. I walked up to her and asked her name.

'Suravi Dey.'

'Can I take your picture?' I asked her. She did not say anything but continued to look at me. I ventured a click without waiting for her approval. She carefully avoided a smile. But when we took our leave of her, we saw her smile feebly.

Before leaving, I posted a parting shot to Bharati. 'You say the sex worker's job should be seen at par with other jobs. So will they be taking a holiday tomorrow for May Day?'

Bharati laughed at my question. 'It is when other workers take leave that these workers find maximum employment. So how can they take leave on May Day?' It was evident she had not liked my question at all.

Bharati De's laughter remained fresh in my mind when we returned to Sonagachi the next day to click some pictures of the unfortunate 'workers' who had to work on May Day. I told the cab driver in advance he should slow down near Sonagachi. He responded with a sly smile and called out well ahead of Sonagachi, 'Be prepared.'

When we saw the women who were all made-up and waiting for customers, the driver slowed down the car so much that it didn't feel like we were moving at all. I clicked continuously, sometimes focusing, sometimes not. As soon as some of the women noticed us, they ran inside the closest building, pointing us out to their friends as they did so. Suddenly, a beautiful girl wearing a tight white T-shirt ran towards our cab, brandishing something and yelling expletives. We heard a heavy thud. Something hit the door of the cab. My camera shook, and my head grew numb. I couldn't figure out what had happened. The driver quickly raised the speed and stopped only after quite a distance to check the damage. Whatever the girl had thrown, it had scraped some yellow paint from the door. The driver smiled while belting out expletives. I comforted myself that they were meant for the girl. He demanded a fare of 70 rupees. We paid him a 100. He smiled and murmured an expletive again.

We gathered the courage to return to Sonagachi the next day. This time, we walked in through a lane that was not crowded by the women soliciting customers. We took care to ensure neither of our faces betrayed any signs of unfamiliarity.

It was at this time that we came upon Anamika Banerjee. Anyone would have been astounded to meet someone like her in a place like this. In her sixties now, she looked nothing like a sex worker, with her dignified bearing, fair face and rounded figure. We introduced ourselves as from the press. The dignity in her appearance was present in her behaviour too. She went to a closed shop, sat in front of it and asked us to sit down next to her.

Anamika said she had been in Sonagachi for more

than 10 years. 'My hometown was in north Bengal. The conditions at home were beyond pathetic. My father was a farmhand, and the money was hardly enough. A broker from our village approached my father saying since I was beautiful, I could have a good future in movies. He said he had some friends in the film industry who could help me get a break. Even watching a movie was a big deal for my parents at the time, and they were delighted by the opportunity that had opened up before me. Kolkata was a place they hadn't even dreamt of visiting. The broker then brought me to Kolkata. Every morning we would go to help me get a break. We would go to Tollygunge studios, and he would introduce me to various people. I used to dress myself up really well, hoping I would get a chance in cinema. But those trips were in vain. Months passed by. I didn't get a single opportunity. Soon, things got so bad I could not manage to get three meals a day. That was when another broker who had been noticing me came and told me about Sonagachi. He was the one who opened up the path to Sonagachi.'

'What did he tell you about this place before he brought you here?' I enquired.

'He told me it was stupidity to expect a chance in the movies. Even if that worked out, I wouldn't get paid. On the other hand, I would have a regular income in Sonagachi and he would arrange accommodation for me here. That's how I came here.

'Sonagachi was like heaven. Food was the most important thing. On most days, I would get work. Even if I didn't get work, I would get food. Being unable to see the outside world is a problem only for those who are used to eating good food every day. For those who have known only hunger, this doesn't matter. Starvation haunts them. Then one day, a Mumbai zamindar somehow took a fancy to me and took me with him to Mumbai after paying the agent generously. He sent me back after a few months, but I had made a few contacts in Mumbai by then. That was helpful too. Some acquaintances from Mumbai ask for me even now. I am also the branch secretary of the Durbar Mahila Samanwaya Committee now.'

'You are beautiful even now,' I said. She was thrilled by that. Suddenly she remembered she had not served us tea. She invited us to have tea at the clinic-office, where she introduced us to a few other sex workers, among them a girl called Parvati from near Rajahmundry in Andhra. She didn't tell us the exact place since she grew worried we may have come from there.

Nonetheless, Parvati told us her story.

After her *kannerakam* was done, the zamindar who had purchased her avoided her, and another acquaintance brought her to Sonagachi. That was in 1990. Parvati told us about several other girls from Andhra who had similar fates as hers, some who had even been sold by the zamindars. But the more she told us, the more she looked worried, and we could see that. Most of the girls did not want to dwell on their past in any case. They preferred to talk about the organization. The Durbar clinic also had facilities for blood tests as well as basic healthcare. The organization had arranged for medical insurance for workers, who can also draw money from this fund when they are unwell. Parvati said, 'We train girls who are new here. If they are minors, we move them to our shelter. We will never allow minor girls to work. We also protect those girls who have been deceived into this by transferring them to the shelter. If the police find lost girls, they call us up and hand them over to us.'

While we were clicking photographs of the sex workers, a woman posed with them, unaware of who we were. The other women explained she was not a sex worker but their nurse.

'Is there anybody from Kerala in your group?' we asked.

'Surely yes. But sorry, we cannot bring them in front of you.' Anamika did not want them to be identified by us since we were from Kerala too.

I thought I should have a word with the clinic's oldest inmate, a 70-year-old woman. She had come to Sonagachi very early in her life, and now she trained the new girls and spread awareness.

'Don't you feel the need to have a family at this age?' I asked her.

'Not at all,' she replied calmly. 'I am always busy here. New girls come in all the time. What's more, if someone asks me, I am ready for work too.'

I was astounded. I looked at her silver-grey hair and wrinkled hands and did not say anything.

I wanted to get a panoramic shot of Sonagachi from the clinic's terrace. I figured that if I could get permission to shoot within the clinic, I could coax them to allow me onto the terrace.

Anamika agreed, and when I went upstairs after clicking some pictures of the clinic, a woman accompanied us. Several hardboard boxes full of condoms were piled up on the staircase. I wondered why they couldn't move the boxes to the rooms, only to discover the rooms were also filled with the same boxes. Five floors up, the terrace opened up. As I expected, it provided a breathtaking view of Sonagachi. I was reminded of Bharati De's remark that there were around 1,083 buildings, big and small, in Sonagachi with 12,118 sex workers in them.

The woman who accompanied me reeled out the names of the lanes that we could see – Manjith Badi Street, Avinash Kabiraj Street, Durgacharan Mitra Street, Shashi Shankar Lane, Rabindra Sarani, Imam Burs Lane etc. Women and children lined all of them.

'Was Sonagachi always this expansive?' I asked her.

'Yes,' she replied. 'With more girls coming in, it has perhaps become more crowded. But however many girls come here, they will get work. All by the beneficence of Kali.'

'Do you believe in god?' I asked.

'All the girls here will spontaneously believe in Kali, irrespective of whether they are from Nepal or Bangladesh.'

'Why hasn't Kali rescued you then?'

'Kali saved us by bringing us here. We are as dear as life to her. To Kali, we prostitutes are of prime importance. Everything else is secondary. Even the Kumortuli sculptors begin making the Kali sculptures for Durga Puja after taking a handful of mud from Sonagachi. Else Kali will be angry. We are everything to Kali, everything.'

We went back to Sonagachi around 10 p.m. the next night to see what the nights were like here. Women and young girls had already lined up on the footpaths by then, trying their gimmicks – making noises and cooing – on whoever passed by. We paused, wondering whether we would get hijacked again like the other day if we went inside the lanes at that time. Suddenly, I felt a hand on my shoulder. I turned around to see a beautiful woman, biting her lips and gesturing at me.

'Come inside. Why do you hesitate?' she asked in Hindi.

I feared other women would gather around us. Thankfully though, sensing our disinterest, she moved to another prey.

'I think it'll be dangerous to go inside without an agent,' Pramod advised. 'Let us find one before she comes back.' He pointed at a man who leaned on a car bonnet a little away. His name was Raama, and he had been an agent in Sonagachi for 20 years now.

'We need a girl for two hours. No one should come in to trouble us or kidnap us,' we instructed him.

'I can take you inside without any harm, but two men with one girl...' he trailed off with an air of doubt. 'There is no dearth of girls, so why are you being stingy?' he asked.

'We just want to talk to her,' I said.

He laughed aloud, as if I had cracked a joke. Then he quietly walked inside. We followed him.

The yellow hue of the street lights gave a peculiar seductive glow to Sonagachi at night. All the women looked like they had freshly bathed and decked up. This was not so in the day. It made sense. After all, the women's day begins at night. We passed by these beauties, our eyes fixed on Raama. Some of them picked on me as I followed last: 'Come, sir.' I pointed at Raama and gestured that I was with him. 'Raama, why don't you give us some clients too? We too have "it",' one woman yelled out in Bengali. The others laughed aloud.

About 20 metres ahead, we arrived at a five-storeyed building fortified by grills on its windows. Raama walked inside and asked us to follow him. There was a long veranda inside, and at one end, an old woman washed her dishes. We had hardly walked two feet when we came upon two rooms. In one, girls were getting ready. One applied make-up, the other was in the process of wearing a sari, assisted by a third girl wearing jeans. They were all in a hurry.

In the next room, a huge, scary-looking woman lay on a bed, wearing a nightie. She chewed paan and angrily abused the girls in the other room who were late for work. The girls sped up as her torrent of abuse increased. She stopped when she saw us approach.

'Raama, ask them to sit inside.' She got ready to play the humble hostess. Raama went inside and talked to her in low tones, while we waited outside.

'We normally charge up to 5,000 rupees for two hours. Since Raama brought you in, I will reduce the price to half and give you one girl each,' she first said.

'We only want one girl,' I said.

'That is up to you, but you need to pay me for two,' she said gruffly.

'We only want to watch her dance. We will not do anything else,' I pleaded.

She was hard to convince but finally settled for a thousand reluctantly, albeit with several warnings. 'Don't you dare touch her. Just sit and watch her decently. If I hear that you have laid a finger on her...'

Before we could say anything, she called out, 'Sandhya!'

A good-looking woman in a sari, who looked to be

about 30, entered. The perfume she wore enveloped the room with its heady fragrance. Her scarlet lips added to her allure. She smiled at us and went to her boss. They discussed something for a few seconds, after which she came to us with a seductive smile. The boss stretched out her hand for payment. We gave her the amount. Raama drew our attention with a smile intended to remind us of his due. We gave him a hundred rupees. He pocketed the note after touching it to his eyes.

'Come,' Sandhya said, smiling coyly as she led us upstairs. We walked up to the third floor. There was no one in the rooms here except a few girls getting dressed in one or two rooms.

Sandhya led us inside a room and latched the door. Apart from a bed, there was a stool. A music system sat on one side and speakers on the other. There was a picture of Kali on top of the door. I asked her to sit on the stool.

'How will I dance then? Let me change my clothes and come,' she said.

I followed the same tactic as with Diya. 'Let's have a beer first.'

She liked that. 'Can we get a pack of cigarettes too?' she asked freely.

'We don't smoke. You can get one if you want.'

She opened the door and called out for cigarettes and beer. Then she sat back on the stool and switched between different songs.

She asked about our names and where we had come from. When she heard we were from Kerala, she grew thoughtful. She closed her eyes for some time and then opened them to reveal a multitude of emotions in them.

'A friend of mine has gone to Kerala. Maybe you can find him for me,' she shyly said and looked at us with hope.

'All Bengalis seem to be working in Kerala these days. We have more Bengalis than our own people there now,' Pramod tried to exaggerate and lighten the mood, but she didn't understand. Or was she lost in some other thought? She didn't speak for a while, until there was a knock at the door. A boy around 20 years old walked in. He placed the beer and glasses on the table and gave her the cigarettes. He cracked some joke at which she laughed heartily and then pushed him out by the nape of his neck. Then she quickly closed the door and sat with us on the bed.

I noticed a window behind the bed. The curtain was half open, and we could see the road below where Sonagachi had come alive with its nightly pleasures. Men approached the women, began to bargain, then finally some walked in together to the buildings in the vicinity.

Following my gaze, Sandhya also looked and said, 'They are there waiting for the last catch of the day.'

'When does duty start for women here?' I asked.

'Pretty much 24/7, but the real rush starts after 7 p.m.'

'Then why were all of you late today? When we came in, you were only getting ready.'

'We had sent off the first three customers. We have to bathe after each one of them. Don't you know that you should visit Kali only when pure? It is the same with customers. We have to bathe before making them happy.'

I looked outside again. Some women now walked away with their customers, while those remaining grew desperate to get one last customer.

Sandhya seemed to be curious about Kerala – how far it was? What could one see there? She asked us questions with a sense of freedom and ease, as though she was our customer and not the other way around. We played along as we wanted her to return the favour. She poured out beer for herself. I asked her how she had ended up in Sonagachi. She began to recount her story as if she was talking to a close friend.

'I come from Murshidabad. My parents were beedi workers. I was thirteen when someone approached them with a marriage proposal. In those parts, girls are married off very early. The proposal came from a man who was already married and had children, but he did not demand dowry, which was a great relief to my parents. They could not afford any dowry for me. I had two younger sisters, and to provide dowry for all three of us was impossible even if our house was sold – which was in any case one room with logs stacked up in place of walls. Anyone offering to marry us without dowry was god in my parents' eyes, so they married me off to that "god" who turned out to be the devil. As soon as he married me, he left his first wife at her place. Then, before a year was over, he himself brought her to Kolkata and sold her in Sonagachi. She thought she would get a job in Kolkata.

'Four years later, I gave birth to a boy. One year later, my husband married again. I met the same fate as the first wife and was brought here. Initially, I had no clue why I was here. The woman you met below is the one who bought me. She told me I should learn how to dance, and some others here taught me. To be honest, I had always wanted to learn how to dance, but my condition at home did not allow me. Now, because of goddess Kali, my wish was fulfilled.' Her eyes misted over when she said this, but she covered it up and got up, saying it was time for her to dance.

'Wait,' I said, 'there is no hurry. Can't you go back home?'

'What for?' She laughed like she had heard a funny joke. 'Don't I get food here? Should I go back home to starve?'

'Are you content?'

'Food is the main problem, and I get it here,' she tried to be evasive.

'But with no one to love you and no one for you to love...' I left my words hanging.

A slight smile played on her lips. 'There was someone to love me here. His name was Sushant, and he had come to Kolkata for construction work. We met a year ago when he came to Sonagachi for the first time. After that, he came frequently and only wanted me. I told him my life story just like I told you. He was the one who told me about Kerala. He said he had found a good job in Kerala and called me several times after going there. But now, it's been three months without any news from him. He said he would take me there. I know Kerala is near Madras. Maybe you can help me find him.'

She looked at us hopefully. I tried telling her Kerala was not as small a place as she had imagined, but she could not understand. She drank some more and spoke about finding Sushant. Changing the topic, I asked her, 'Where is your son now?'

'He is at home. Didi arranges to send some money to him every month. Because he is a boy, he won't end up like me. I am lucky to have Kali with me. I told you, I wanted to learn dance. Kali fulfilled my wishes by bringing me here. Now, I will dance for you.' She jumped up and started swaying to the music. She asked us to excuse her if she was not very good, as she was not used to dancing in a sari. But I thought her movements had the mark of a well-trained dancer. When I looked down the window again, I could see few women now, just a handful who looked older.

After the song finished, she took a break. 'Shall I take your picture?' I asked her. I had previously heard stories of how people were beaten up for smuggling in cameras inside Sonagachi.

'You have a camera? Quickly, take my picture,' she said, taking me by surprise. I clicked three to four pictures quickly before she changed her mind. When she saw her pictures, she grew excited. Then she teared up and asked if we could record her dancing as well. I discouraged her by saying our time was almost over. In reality, I feared the menacing woman would walk in and spot the camera.

'Give me another 200, and I will buy us time for another hour,' she said. No sooner had we given her the money than she ran down.

While she was away, we stepped outside to get some fresh air. It was now past midnight. Some women waited by the street even now. The loud sounds of bargaining and the general hubbub of the evening had died out. All that could be heard was the sound of cars zipping past. Even the shreds of light coming out of the ancient buildings of Sonagachi were dying down. But the women stood still, ready with their smiles to welcome a last customer.

As we stood there watching all this, we heard a groaning sound and looked around. There was no light in any room on our floor other than ours. The other rooms were locked from the inside. We followed the sound to a few feet away from us, where I saw an old woman lying in a corner of the veranda. When I tried to look at her using the mobile phone's torch, she expressed discomfort. We turned the light away from her and asked her why she was there.

'Please don't come near me. You can get young women. I am really old.'

I grew disturbed to think this old woman had thought

we were approaching her for sex.

'We have come for Sandhya. Is this where you sleep?' I asked with concern.

'You do your job and leave!' she screamed at us. 'I was also in one of these rooms years ago, when I was younger and made men happy. But when I turned old and unwanted, they kicked me out. I don't have a place to sleep today. All these girls here will face the same fate when they grow old. Even your Sandhya will have to sleep here someday.'

By then, Sandhya returned. She took us inside and bolted the door. She wanted one more photo of hers. Once that was done, she wanted me to record her dance. Then she excitedly watched the whole video. She seemed enchanted by her own movements. She insisted on another recording, then another. Finally, after six recordings, she gathered her breath. I picked the moment to ask her about the woman outside. She said there were several like her here and that we should not invite trouble by enquiring about them.

'But ultimately you will also end up like her, won't you?'

'Maybe. But at least my son will be spared. What if I had had a girl? Wouldn't she end up in the same hellhole? So many women here have had to initiate their daughters into this horrible life. They would all have feared for them just like her when they turned old and then had to endure great pain in isolation. The thought of their daughters' miserable future double their miseries. Thankfully, I don't have a daughter to worry about. Kali is with me. That is how you could see my dance too. I told you...'

Before Sandhya could finish, there was a knock on the door. She jumped up, grabbed the cigarette box and put a cigarette each into both our mouths, taking a third for herself before opening the door. It was the huge woman, her face contorted with doubt and suspicion.

'They will leave as soon as they finish the cigarette,' Sandhya said.

'Hmm.' Didi's grunt did not sound happy at all.

The moment she moved away from the door, Sandhya closed the door without latching it and threw the cigarettes and the matchbox on the bed. Then she took the camera from me and handed it to Pramod, asking him to take a picture of us together. Pramod hesitated, fearing her boss had not left the floor. But Sandhya wasn't willing to let go. 'Quickly, quickly!' she said in hushed undertones. Pramod's hands were shivering as he clicked some pictures. She asked me why I was so scared. I realized I too had been shivering. Sandhya then looked at the pictures and hurriedly gave the camera to me and posed with Pramod for a picture. I peeped through the keyhole and saw Didi in the corner of the veranda. I quickly managed three or four pictures.

In an instant, I showed them to Sandhya and then immediately hid the camera in my pocket.

She opened the door, and we walked down, Sandhya and Didi walking in single file behind us. When we reached the ground floor, Sandhya shook our hands and said, 'If you are able to find my friend...' But before she could finish, I told her it was unlikely we would find him without any details about his whereabouts. Then she said, 'If he ever takes me to Kerala with him, we will meet again.' She smiled, hoping against hope, a listless smile.

Ten or twelve girls now occupied the room where we had seen the girls get ready earlier in the night. They slept in various places and poses – on the chairs, on the bed and on the floor.

We bid goodbye to Didi. She grunted her displeasure once more. Sandhya waved at us. There was no one on the road now, and we had not imagined Sonagachi could be as abandoned as that. A little further, Sandhya called out to us. We turned around to see her waving us bye. We returned the gesture. Raama remained in the same position as before on the main road.

'Didn't you go?' I asked him.

'I stay here till 3 a.m. You never know when people will come. When they do, they should not experience any inconvenience. That's why I am here, sacrificing my sleep,' Raama revealed his professional commitment.

Before getting into a taxi, I took one last look at Sonagachi. Though the place was home to thousands of beautiful women, I felt there was no beauty in its soul.

# 8

# Kalighat, Whose Sins Refuse to Be Washed Off

I HAVE ALREADY MENTIONED THAT KOLKATA GOT ITS NAME from Kalighat. This is a place located a little away from the city and named Kalighat because of the Kali temple.

The river Adi Ganga flows next to the temple, the river's name meaning 'original Ganga'. Perhaps the generations of people who have washed off their sins here have rendered the Adi Ganga as putrid as a sewage channel today. The road to the Kalighat temple was a riot of colours. Powders in different colours that are offered to the goddess were scattered all over. The dogs on the street and the children who begged for alms had all acquired a colourful aura. Ironically, their lives seemed to be bereft of colour.

The Kalighat police station is next to the temple. As we walked down the lane beside it, several women approached us when they realized we were visitors: 'Do you want some, sir? We will reduce the price for you.'

We walked ahead, pretending to hear nothing, and noticed a lanky old woman sitting away from the others. When we told her we were journalists, without hesitation she asked us to sit down. Listening to her, we felt she had been yearning for long to confide in someone.

Her name was Mira, and according to her, it was the abolition of sati that turned Kalighat into a locality of sex workers. Her mother, Debjani, came from north Bengal, where the sati tradition had been deep-rooted. Debjani was wedded at 12 and widowed at 20. If she had been born earlier, she would have had to jump into her husband's pyre. Although sati had been banned by then, there were several people in those parts who wished the custom to continue.

According to her, the banning of sati made things more difficult for women. 'Earlier on, a widow's problems would come to an end by plunging into the husband's pyre, and thus they were spared further misery. The practice also bestowed upon the women instant divinity posthumously. Temples would be built at the spot where sati was observed, and pujas would be conducted in the widows' names. But when the ban came, people began looking at widows as criminals. They were scared to insist on sati for fear of being penalized, but they forced the widows out of their homes nonetheless. Village landlords then advised them to go live on the banks of the Ganga as a kind of penance for the sin of widowhood. My mother would say this was also an escape in a way because if they were to stay on in the village, they would have to live as concubines of the men of the family. No one dared remarry a widow as it was considered a horrible sin. If the widow thought about moving back to her parents' home, her siblings would not approve of it. The widows would be ostracized as no one would invite a family that supported a widow to auspicious functions. In such situations, it was better to take refuge in a temple. This was how widows came to live on the banks of the Adi Ganga in huge numbers in those days.

'My mother reached Kalighat in 1940. She would beg for alms near the temple. There were hundreds of widows like her by then at Kalighat. The rich people who came here would invite these widows to share their beds. They would stay near the temple at night and leave after *darshan* early in the morning. Before their prayers, they craved carnal desires too. Honestly speaking, it is not by the grace of god but by the "blessings" of these devotees that the widows at Kalighat managed to survive. Many had regular "devotees". They would come once or twice a month for *darshan* and give some money when they left.

'Slowly, one widow would be replaced by another. After all, new widows came in every day. Eventually, the widows turned to full-fledged prostitution as livelihood. That is how my mother became a sex worker.'

Mira herself was born in 1944. She didn't know who her

father was. Her childhood was spent begging at the temple premises. One day, after she had attained puberty, her mother came with some men and asked her to go with one of them. She had no idea what for. That was her initiation into sex work. She said several widows had taken refuge in Banaras too, and prostitution was their chief occupation as well. We felt if we asked around, several other women would have the same story.

Leaving Mira behind, we headed to the NGO New Light's office. The lane was besieged by women. A condom-vending machine was installed there. Since the women at Kalighat were not as well-informed as the ones at Sonagachi, NGOs had installed these vending machines. When they saw us looking closely at the vending machine, some of the women got hopeful. 'Saabji, saabji,' they called out as they followed us. We said no and added a few keywords such as 'reporter' and 'newspaper', but they did not seem to hear it. When they finally realized we weren't interested in their services, they turned around.

After several bends and turns along the narrow lane, we finally reached the New Light office, which was on the top floor of a dilapidated building. But from our conversations at the office, we realized we couldn't learn anything new than what Urmi had already told us. So we retraced our steps, noticing that several of the women whom we had seen while walking in had been replaced by others. We assumed they would have found customers.

It was ironic that the sacred Ganga, no more than a dirty canal here, which is supposed to purge away sins, had been swamped by other sins right on its banks. Broken idols littered the riverbank, with pots and garlands dumped as part of various rituals. We crossed over to the other bank on two boats that had been tied together. Here too, there were lines of small huts and small, treacherous lanes in between. As we navigated through them, we could see women in all the huts, who were getting ready for the night. We approached a middle-aged woman who had the same story as those on the other side. When we asked her about this place's history, however, she said, 'Who cares about history? Isn't it more important to find sustenance every day?'

I realized the truth of what she was saying. I could see several women getting ready for the night ahead. Several held cigarettes in their hands, probably to counter the boredom of waiting. When they saw us approaching, they would pause for a while and stare. On realizing we were not what they were looking for, they put the cigarettes back to their lips. They seemed to truly enjoy the act of smoking, and the way they let out the smoke would make anyone envious. We weaved through the rings of smoke back to the Adi Ganga, which had ingested all the smoke and sin and turned black.

Before leaving Kolkata, we thought we must visit Kumortuli, where the sculptors who make the idols for Durga Puja live. The preparations for the festival had started, and most of them were too busy to talk to us. When I asked some about the practice of taking mud from Sonagachi, they claimed not to know anything about it. I wondered if the women at Sonagachi were making up stories and if this had been their way of laying claim to history.

A sculptor named Suraj, however, explained, 'There was such a tradition long ago. We used to get the first fistful of mud from Sonagachi before making the idols in a ceremony. The belief was that the mud outside a prostitute's house would be full of virtue. When a man enters a prostitute's house, he leaves his virtues outside. Hence, the mud outside is accumulated with all the good that men have. The tradition was practised till recently. However, things have changed in Sonagachi. It has become a place where girls are traded with no ethics. No decent man would go there. Therefore, we decided to move on with the times and not practise it any longer.'

Many of the sculptors were digging mud out from pits for the idols. Listening to Suraj's tale, I couldn't help feeling these pits also buried within them multi-layered narratives of faith and history.

# 9

# Jalangi of Boundless Poverty

A FIVE-HOUR-RIDE FROM KOLKATA BRINGS US TO Murshidabad, the headquarters of the eponymous district which shares its borders with Bangladesh. The town has the unique and undesirable distinction of being ranked the poorest place in the country by the Statistical Survey of India. We stepped out of the railway station into the first food stall that caught the eye. The shopkeeper, Manohar Dutta, received us respectfully upon learning we were journalists from Kerala. He said a lot of his fellow Bengalis could sustain themselves only because they worked in Kerala. He was aware that the CPM was a leading party in Kerala and advised us to study why West Bengal had not achieved any credible progress or economic development despite a three-decade-long CPM rule. He started reeling out facts and figures like a seasoned economist – starting with the illegal immigration from Bangladesh. Pramod whispered that encouraging him to talk would be of use as we could get more details about the town.

We told him that when we learnt most sex workers in Sonagachi had come from Murshidabad, we had come to the town to enquire why it was so. Manohar then launched into the topic like an expert. 'The biggest curse of people here is that they are not educated. Kerala's blessing is that it has achieved widespread and equitable progress in education. Most girls here study up to the sixth or seventh standard, or in some rare cases, up to the tenth. Boys drop out even before. Girls are married off by the age of 18, and by 20 they become mothers. The men always find ways to get new girls. So they marry another girl and drop off the older wife at Sonagachi or other red-light areas. Further, parents are forced to give off their unmarried daughters to married men because they cannot afford a huge dowry to get a decent young man as a husband. They hardly have any options. In some cases, the parents themselves send off their girls to Sonagachi because of their absolute poverty.'

I told him we wanted to gather some details from the India–Bangladesh border town of Jalangi. Urmi Basu's allegation that the BSF aided the trafficking of Bangladeshi girls to India in Jalangi played on my mind. Manohar then gave us the precise directions to go to the border town by bus. The Chunakhali Nimtala junction was five kilometres from Murshidabad, and we had to ride a bus for an hour and a half from there to reach Jalangi. George Bruno, a friend who worked for the rights of migrant labourers, had earlier informed us that the Sarkar Pada Street in Jalangi was home to the families of many labourers who had either died or been injured while employed in Kerala. In Jalangi, we walked to Sarkar Pada, a kilometre away from the bus stand, noticing a BSF camp en route.

Most of the homes in Sarkar Pada were just two rooms made of jute sticks. Some homes had tiled roofs, while a few had concrete roofing. I realized later that the homes that looked reasonably better belonged to labourers working in Kerala.

On hearing that we were from Kerala and had come to see the injured workers, Jatin Mundol, who was employed in Kerala and had come home on holiday, volunteered to help us. With his assistance, we covered several houses. When I told Jatin that Bengalis did not have a good reputation in Kerala because Bangladeshis also claimed to be Indian Bengalis, Jatin agreed with me. He asserted that Bangladeshis were responsible for all the theft and murders in Kerala and because of them Bengalis had unfortunately borne the brunt of the disrepute. I then asked about the allegations that girls were being trafficked into Kolkata via this route. Jatin agreed. He said that there were some girls who were forcefully brought in, while others came on their own to escape the dire poverty in Bangladesh.

'How do they manage to cross over so easily?' Pramod, who worked in the BSF, asked.

'Well, there is no fencing at the border,' Jatin said.

'But there is the BSF, isn't there?' I asked.

'That is easy to overcome,' he dismissed our concerns easily.

We asked him if we could go to the border and see for ourselves. He was more than happy to oblige and led the way. The border here is demarcated by the Padma River, and the way to it was through a ridge that bordered jute fields, creating a narrow path. We could finally see the Padma River before us in all its glory, reflecting the afternoon sun like a huge crystal slab. Beyond the river, we could make out oceans of green fields. What the river lacked in depth and strength of current, it made up for in its width and grandeur.

The British had zeroed in on the Padma River as part of their master plan to separate Bengal and through it the minds of a nation and its people in the name of religion. The river that had once been the lifeline of several cultures and lives suddenly turned into a never-ending source of tears and pain once the border was created. The wounds of Partition then created a river of blood here. Later, when Bangladesh was born, this river continued to sever the two countries.

We walked to the BSF watchtower, where we met two *jawans*, one from Andhra Pradesh and the other from Kashmir. Instructions came in monotone static on their walkie talkie as we spoke to them. We told them we had come to enquire about labourers and that we were just visiting the border as it was close by. Pramod asked them how difficult it was to stay away from their families. They seemed to be delighted to find listeners to their story and turned out to be far more loquacious than we had expected.

After we had heard their sorrows, I told them about the allegation that several Bangladeshis had taken this route across the border to go as far south as Kerala and that girls were also being trafficked on this route.

The soldier from Andhra said, 'If Bangladeshis are crossing the border illegally, it is with the help of the Bengalis, without doubt. Bengalis bring them across, claiming they are family or friends. But when these guys commit a crime somewhere, Bengalis will complain that they are being misunderstood. If girls are reaching Kolkata, that is impossible without the help of locals. They mislead us by telling us stories of family and kin and bring the girls across for a commission. They have no idea where the girls will end up.'

Jatin Mundol completely agreed with the *jawan*, although it was contrary to what he had said earlier.

'People here forge fake ID cards for the Bangladeshis as soon as they cross over,' the *jawan* added, and Jatin agreed to that too.

The soldiers allowed us to take pictures of the river from the watchtower while warning us not to click their pictures.

We did so and retraced our steps. On the way back, Jatin was once again voluble about Bangladeshis and their misdeeds. He had forgotten the strong allegations made by the *jawan*s just a few minutes ago.

# 10

# The Radhas of Vrindavan

I HAD MADE UP MY MIND TO VISIT VRINDAVAN THE moment Urmi Basu told us about widows from Bengal ending up there. Vrindavan is about ten kilometres before Mathura, and one can see several huge temples along this route. It was quite obvious that these temples decided where the bus stopped here. The only mantra that resounds all over Vrindavan is that of 'Radhe Radhe', which is not merely a chant that is repeated in devotional fervour here but also a way to ask people to move aside and give way or as to greet people. In effect, 'Radhe Radhe' occupies a central space in the communication matrix within Vrindavan.

Vrindavan is revered as the spot where Krishna spent his childhood years, as per the mythology. No wonder it is surrounded by plenty of temples. The Bankebihari Maharaj temple is the most prominent of them all and also the most crowded. As we walked past the streets early morning, I thought there were more temples than homes here and more ashrams for *sanyasinis* than tea stalls. The ashrams announced their presence with colourful boards and looked well maintained, even more so than the temples.

We noticed a cot was placed outside almost all the homes beside the road, the purpose of which was unknown to us. When we told a guide named Hari that we were on the trail of Krishna devotees referred to as Radhas, Hari said that there were at least 10,000 Radhas in Vrindavan, all of whom were engaged in bhajans every morning and evening.

'Bhajans?' I asked.

'Yes. The Radhas have to praise Lord Krishna, don't they? The lord is their husband.'

Only then we realized why we hadn't seen any Radhas till then. They would be busy with bhajans till 9 a.m.

The heat was bearable in the morning, so we explored Vrindavan on foot. We noticed that Radha, Krishna's consort, was given more importance than Krishna in almost all the temples. At the Nidhivan Sevadhikari temple, there was even a 'Shringar Ghar' set up for Radha. A 'Shringar Ghar' is where sleeping chambers and other personal accoutrements for the deity are recreated. In places, the priests allow devotees to see the 'Shringar Ghar' only from the outside, but here, if we gave the priest 25 rupees, we were allowed to go inside and see it up close. Devotees consider it a big honour to touch the bedding of Radha and Krishna.

The Mirabai Bhajan Ashram near the temple was essentially one big hall. On either end were some wooden cupboards, with five or six sections that seemed to be apportioned among the Radhas to keep their clothes. Female devotees of Krishna are known as Radhas here. In scripture, Radha the gopika was Krishna's beloved when he lived in Vrindavan, and she is believed to be the personification of devotion to Krishna.

Mats were folded in front of the cupboards for the Radhas to sleep at night. Another corner of the ashram was screened with a cupboard that served as the store. The food grains allotted to each Radha were apparently stored here. We were told all the ashrams followed a similar structure, the only difference being the size of the hall, which would vary depending on the number of inhabitants. About a hundred women lived in the Mirabai Ashram. Most of them sat in groups. We noticed an older lady who sat by herself in front of the Krishna statue and sang. We didn't want to disturb her devotion, but she took note of us even as she sang and gestured to us to come near her. She then invited us to pray to the lord. We remained there till her song receded to a mere hum. Soon, she stopped humming and began to speak with us.

Her name was Padma Dasi. Her parents had been daily wage labourers in Nabadwip in Bengal, and she had been married off at the age of 14. Soon after, however, she felt the 'calling' to see Krishna. She arrived in Vrindavan with her husband and had lived here since then. She said that her husband stayed in another ashram close by and visited her every now and then.

Padma was proud of being able to sing for her lord for three hours every morning and evening. Though she spoke eloquently about her life, something about her made me feel she was trying to hide something.

'What about your children?' I asked her.

'Everything belongs to Lord Krishna. I do not think of anything now. I have nothing of my own,' she said. I thought she was being evasive.

When I asked about their financial situation back in Nabadwip, she gave a sketchy answer. 'Perhaps there were several miseries long back, but Krishna has saved us from all of those.' She then sighed and continued to chant 'Radhe Radhe', before singing the rest of the hymn she had been singing earlier. She hinted that she got five rupees for singing the bhajans. Then she raised her singing pitch, as if to make it amply clear she did not want to be disturbed by further questions. A group of women had been observing us, so we moved towards them. When we took out the camera, all of them grew delightfully curious and started posing for us cheerfully. The oldest among them was Bhagwati, who was 75 and was also from Bengal. Her husband had been a daily wage labourer in Nadia district. Work had become so scarce they had almost starved. Her husband would work in neighbouring villages, but after a point even that had stopped. All the widows from that region went to Vrindavan, and Bhagwati also began to be tempted by the thought that they could get three meals a day here. So although she wasn't a widow, she also took a bus one day and came here. She hardly had money for the bus ticket and had to switch several buses before she arrived in Vrindavan.

'How is it here?' I asked her.

'We don't have to starve here,' she said with great relief. 'The ashrams give us 10 rupees every day to sing bhajans, and we use that to buy food. We also get a pension of 450 rupees per month from the government.'

'Don't you feel sad?' I gently probed her.

'Sadness… why? What for?' she asked and then turned her head away. The women in the group refused to talk to us after that.

We realized that the Radhas would not open up to strangers like us very easily, so we decided to go to the District Legal Service Authority, which has been entrusted by the Supreme Court since August 2011 with the responsibility of studying and reporting the socio-economic conditions of the Radhas in Vrindavan. We got in touch with Gaurav Sharma, who was the chairman of the organization in Mathura. He sent us two volunteers – Satish Chandra Sharma and Varun Kumar Sharma.

The two told us that the intervention of the legal services authority had greatly improved the condition of the women in Vrindavan. 'They did not get food and other supplies regularly earlier. Thousands of women come here from Nadia, Midnapore and Nabadwip. They moved here after the ban on sati. The social mindset of their villages had not progressed enough to assimilate widows into their society. They were not allowed to participate in any auspicious functions. The social ostracism could be bearable to some extent, but when their own families and even the children began to ostracize them, they were truly shattered. That is when they came here. Plus, the fact that this a holy place also attracted them. After all, it is a blessing to die here. Then other women also started following the widows here – those who were being tortured by their in-laws or were suffering in poverty. All of them saw Vrindavan as a refuge. They became permanent residents of Vrindavan as Radhas. Though they rush to the temple two times a day for bhajans, their main source of income is begging,' Satish told us.

I asked him about the reports that a few Radhas had died on the streets in the past due to lack of nutritious food and appropriate healthcare. Satish corrected me by saying, 'That has been rectified by the authority. There are now government shelters where multiple NGOs look after the welfare of the women. The authority reports directly to the Supreme Court if there are any discrepancies. Today, no Radhas are homeless or on the roads. They have all been accommodated in shelters. We take care of minute details, including providing for their sanitary requirements. The authority has intervened to ensure regular pensions and supplies as well.'

When we said we would like to see the condition of the Radhas personally, they took us to an area called Chaitanya Vihar. It was noon when we reached, and we could see several shelters run by NGOs to provide for the Radhas. Each shelter was a big hall, where food supplies were kept in a corner, while another worked as the office. The rest of the space was reserved for the Radhas' sleeping arrangements, a little like a general ward in a hospital. Several of the Radhas we saw were ailing patients, lonely and hapless without any family to look after them.

We first met with widows from an organization called Maitri India. Varun and Satish immediately checked the registers and attendance book. There were 161 women here, of whom 31 were not present that day. Some had gone to ashrams, and others had gone to their native villages. The majority of them were Bengalis and others from Odisha and Assam.

As soon as we stepped into their room, the Radhas got up and greeted us with 'Radhe, Radhe'. We returned the greeting. A septuagenarian from West Bengal's 24 Parganas district, named Ranjini Sarkar, was the first one to talk to us. 'Krishna has invited me here as Radha. I wish to die here while serving him,' she said.

'Was life happy back home?'

'Definitely. But that is not enough, isn't it? When one

gets the calling to serve god, it has to be fulfilled at some point.' Her eyes were overflowing with the bliss of devotion.

'Were you a devotee of Krishna from childhood?' I asked.

'No,' she replied.

'When did you start hearing about Krishna?' I asked, my interest piqued.

'After my husband's death, I became isolated in his house. When the isolation became too much to bear, I felt like I should escape somewhere. It was at that time I started hearing about Vrindavan. All the widows in our neighbourhood were boarding buses to Vrindavan. So I joined them. After coming here, I got to learn more about Krishna.'

'Don't you want to go back?' I asked, looking into her eyes.

'Go back from this holy land? Are you crazy? Why would I want to leave this soil where our lord Krishna spent his childhood?' she responded with unconcealed disgust.

'Would you be here if society had not isolated you?'

'Who knows whether the isolation was not part of lord's plans to bring me here?'

I was amazed by her interpretation of her past misery. I probed further, 'Do you have children?'

'Yes. My whole life was a struggle to bring them up. But what's the point? They were the ones who asked me to leave home,' she said, her eyes welling up.

'Are you angry with them?'

'No.' She covered her tearful eyes with her hands. 'When I am happy and satisfied here, why should I think about them?'

'Would you go back if they came and called you home?' I dropped my voice low as I pushed her to the edge.

'I already said I wouldn't.' She paused for a while before continuing again, 'But I do wish they would come and call me home.' She then broke down, and I regretted exposing her efforts to mislead herself and others that she was happy and content with the ecstasy of devotion.

The other Radhas had learnt their lesson seeing Ranjini cry. They then told me they had been guided by the love of Krishna and that they had no other wish but to die in his service. They said they would not return to their children, while admitting they were upset their children had neglected them totally. Like Ranjini, the other women were willing to divulge only stories of their devotion to Krishna, be it the 85-year-old Keerthana Maitra from Midnapore, Tulu Biswas from 24 Parganas, Kamila Behera from Odisha, or others.

'Most of them will die here, won't they?' I asked the warden later.

'Haven't you read the Puranas? It is considered good fortune to die in the soil of Vrindavan. Maybe they will get salvation,' the young warden spoke in Bengali. She explained that she had to learn Bengali as most of the women who came to Vrindavan were Bengalis. 'In their villages they believe that a widow is a cursed woman, and therefore, most of them are shunted out of their homes by their own families. Even the woman's parents may do so.'

Satish then told us they had collected the phone numbers of their families so that they could inform them if a Radha died. If they did not have a family, the cremation would be conducted with appropriate rituals. The government had allocated 3,000 rupees for each cremation, and additionally, the authority had even managed to get a Supreme Court order that all cremations had to be conducted under the supervision of the district medical officer, thus making the process watertight. He added that the Radhas in Vrindavan were proof of the state's open-mindedness and that no action had been taken in West Bengal against the mass exodus of the widows. He also mentioned that the Supreme Court had reprimanded the West Bengal government on this issue several times.

In another shelter in Chaitanya Vihar, run by an NGO called Action Point, we met two women in the office. When Satish told them that he had to check the register, one of them went in and brought another woman with drowsy eyes. She was presumably the person in charge, but she was outright rude to us.

Satish then repeated he wanted to check the register. She replied the inmates would be back only at 9 p.m. so we should come back at that time.

'Let the inmates come whenever they want. How does it matter if I check the registers?' Satish did not relent.

'What right do you have to check the registers here?' the woman retorted.

'We are volunteers of the Legal Services Authority and have been authorized by the Supreme Court.'

'Whoever you may be, you can check only with prior notice, or you may come back at night.' She refused to budge.

Both sides had begun to raise their voices, with Satish and Varun vociferously listing out their right to examine the registers, while the women emphatically denied their right to do so. Finally, Satish called someone on the phone and complained they were not being allowed to inspect the registers, while the woman in charge also called someone and complained they were being harassed on the pretext of inspection. Caught between the shows of belligerence, we stood there nonplussed. Satish hung up the phone and began explaining to us the rules and regulations that have to be followed by such shelters. Then, the woman in charge arrived with her phone and handed it over to Satish, saying the person on the other end wanted to speak to him. As expected, it was an unpleasant conversation, with a lot of cross-questioning regarding the inspection. It ended in mutual disagreement. Satish immediately made another call and handed the phone to her. We could hear her being questioned about why she wasn't allowing the inspection, and the call ended with a warning that higher authorities would arrive there immediately. The woman became so exasperated that she almost threw the phone at Satish, who looked at us triumphantly. 'They will all be here now,' he said.

The woman then brashly ordered her assistants to bring the register and settled down in an armchair. One of them went in and brought out a register after a while and handed it to Satish, who started poring over it sternly. Soon enough, he jumped up with the excitement of a policeman who had spotted a crime.

'See? Including today, they have not taken attendance for three days. Why?' He turned to the ladies.

'We did not have enough time. We don't get paid for working overtime,' one of them retorted.

'No, it's not that you didn't have time. This is for pilferage.' Satish turned to us. 'If these people don't mark attendance, no one will know who is here and who isn't. They can then easily divert the rations to themselves. This is their trick,' he said.

The women remained silent.

While Satish continued explaining the discrepancies he found, a man entered the shelter. 'Are you from the police station?' Satish asked.

'Yes. I am a civil police officer from the Vrindavan Police Station.'

The officer listened patiently to both sides. Satish complained the women had behaved rudely towards him, and to confirm his statement, he asked the officer to check with us.

Then he went outside to make a few more calls. Meanwhile, the cop chastised the women. 'You have to maintain the register. There is no excuse for not doing that.'

The women gave their side of the story. When he advised them they should definitely maintain the register diligently from hereon, they readily agreed.

Satish walked in and announced that the district provisional officer was on his way. The policeman walked out with him. We joined them.

'Why are you fighting with those women? Is it really necessary?' the officer asked Satish. 'There is no need to bring the DPO here. Please tell him not to come. You can also leave after that.'

'We will leave after he comes,' Satish insisted.

The officer left after instructing Satish to inform the DPO he had promptly visited and addressed the complaint. Satish then told us the DPO would arrive soon and as he was an honest man, he would surely take action against the erring staff.

'Shall we visit other shelters in the meantime?' I asked

him, trying to defuse the situation and extricate ourselves from this argument.

'Please wait,' he said. 'You are my witnesses, so wait for him to come.'

We were trapped. Our plan was disrupted, and we had no choice but to wait. Half an hour later, the DPO, Janaprasad, arrived. But instead of coming inside the shelter's office, he stopped at the road that led to the shelters and arranged for chairs to be placed there. We, as witnesses, got separate chairs too. By now, several Radhas had also gathered at the venue after hearing about the incident.

The DPO spoke to everyone and carefully studied the situation. Then he got angry when the shelter worker interrupted him while he was talking to Satish. He rebuked her immediately and warned her not to come up with any explanations if she wasn't asked for them. Then he reprimanded Satish, 'The inspection should be done by responsible people from the authority and not the para-volunteers, right?' In effect, he resolved the situation by being the perfect diplomat, absolving and indicting everyone at the same time.

The DPO finally stood up and hastily declared the problems were solved. Only then did he notice us. He came to us and reiterated there were no problems as we had seen how he had resolved everything.

'Did you come from Mathura?' I asked, just by way of conversation.

'If you have come all the way to Vrindavan from Kerala, can I not come from Mathura?' he tried to flatter us.

The Radhas who had gathered then rushed to him and crowded around him. One group wanted their pensions to be increased. Another complained their supplies were not sufficient. There was no dearth of complaints, but the DPO patiently listened to all of them, perhaps due to our presence. However, when he realized there was no end to the complaints, he looked at his watch, indicating he had no more time to stay back, and made his exit skilfully. Soon after, the Radhas came to us. We were ready to listen to them as it was a new experience for us, but since our two guides had heard them many times over, they started making haste. Eventually we gave in and took leave of the Radhas.

We returned to the crowded streets of Vrindavan at 5 p.m. Bhajan mutts, built exclusively as ashrams to sing bhajans, had come alive by then. These mutts have wide halls just as the ashrams do, the only difference being that there are no cupboards inside the hall. We could see several groups of Radhas heading towards the mutts. There was a pandemonium of salutations to Krishna outside a few. When we took a look inside one, we found it to be filled with Radhas – around 700 of them! The women sat in two large groups and faced each other. Only the women who sat in the front row played the instruments and sang aloud. The others did lip service. Several of the elderly ones dozed off, despite the deafening noise inside:

*Jai nandanandan Gopijan-vallabhan*
*Radhanayak nagarshyam*
*So sachinandan, nadiya purandar*
*Sur munigan, manomohan dham*
*Jai Nijakantha, kanthi kalevar.*

The bhajan continued to progress vigorously to the accompaniment of musical instruments. When I went into their midst to click a picture, several of them looked at me curiously. The lead singers seemed to increase their volume when I approached. The ones behind pretended to sing while looking at me. When I walked out after clicking the pictures, a few of the singers also came out and asked us if we were from the press. When we said yes, a deluge of complaints flooded us: their rations were not enough; they were not getting medical assistance; the pension was too low. All of them said the same things. When I told them we were there to record their way of life and that they should approach the concerned authorities with their issues, they did not agree. 'There is no point talking to the authorities,' they said. 'Only the press can do something about it.'

'But we are from Kerala,' I objected, but that didn't deter them.

'Then get us help from Kerala!'

We left them with some platitudes and went into another mutt. Here, the bhajans were different, but the complaints remained the same. We listened to them for a while, comforted them and then walked out. When there were no other listeners, they went back to their bhajans:

*Hare Krishna Boli Gayite*
*Gayite nayane bahibe lor*
*Dehate pulak, udit*
*Hayive, premete karibe bhor*

Around dusk, we saw several Radhas begging for alms by the roadside, stretching out their arms to anyone who passed. They were looked down upon as a nuisance by everybody who saw them. The majority ignored them and walked past with the air of this being a daily spectacle. A few people dropped some coins for them.

That evening, we met Vinita, a native of Nadia who was very different from the other Radhas we had met so far. Fearless in her approach and with a devil-may-care attitude, she spoke openly with us. 'I was born in Mayapur in Nadia, West Bengal. When I was 14, I was married off to a 50-year-old man. This was about half a century ago, and in those days, such was the custom.

'Young girls would always be married off to older men. The situation at our home was pathetic. Since my marriage would take place with a minimal amount of dowry, my parents also preferred this arrangement. Within a year, I gave birth to a baby boy. A year after that, my husband died. And although sati was banned, most of the villagers wanted the custom to continue; it was only the fear of law that kept them from executing it. I continued to live in my husband's house for three years, wrapped in a white sari. The belief in those parts is that the sin of the woman's vagina causes her husband's death. Thus, the condition of a widow in her husband's house is worse than that of a domestic animal. I was excluded from all auspicious functions and was locked up at home. I was given two meals a day, and even that was not out of any affection or out of compassion but compulsion. After a point, life became unbearable.

'My future looked bleak. I heard about Vrindavan from one of our neighbours, who had been living in Vrindavan. She came home once a year to see her son. She was moved by my plight and advised me to come to Vrindavan with her. When she told me three meals a day were assured, I really didn't have to think about it. My in-laws did not mind it either as the destination was Vrindavan. They were anyway looking to get rid of the liability that I was. So I came here after taking a train and a bus and was accepted into a mutt. There were a hundred other women like me in the mutt. Some had lost their husbands, while others had taken refuge despite having husbands. The guru in charge asked me about my past. After hearing me out, he assured me that there was a solution for everything. "Don't you believe in Krishna?" he asked. I had no choice but to say yes. He told me to become a Radha like the others and said Krishna would take care of everything once I became a Radha. He asked me to learn the bhajans, and I learnt them all from the other Radhas. He would explain the meaning of the bhajans and kirtans every now and then. It was entertaining to listen to his interpretations. The guru would pepper his discourse with stories from his past. One day, he asked me. "How will you love Krishna?" I had no answer to that. "Krishna died ages ago, didn't he? Then how will you marry him?' he asked again. While I pondered it over, he answered for me, "Krishna assumes the form of different avatars at different times. You need to find that avatar." Later, his advice was to try and see Krishna in him. Thus, I started seeing Krishna in him. He was Krishna to several other Radhas too. Who else can be Krishna other than he who provides me with enough food?

'With his death, however, all the Radhas in our mutt became orphaned in a way. If he were here, I wouldn't have to beg like this. Anyway, the sin of my cursed vagina was expiated through the union with my Krishna. Now I am sure to go to heaven. Who else is heaven for if not for people like me who have served Krishna for so long?'

It was frustrating to see how artfully exploitation was being masqueraded as godliness and that these women blinded by belief failed to realize their own plight. Realizing it was pointless to argue, we wished her the best and returned to our hotel. It was on our way back that we met Pooja, who came from Odisha. She had been in love with Krishna even before she ended up in Vrindavan. Her first refuge was a mutt. And because Krishna was everything to her, she was willing to accept the guru of the mutt as her Krishna.

'How would marrying the guru give you access to Krishna?' I asked her curiously.

'To be with Krishna, you need to become someone else's wife first. Only then will Krishna consider us fit to be his lover. Which means if we want to become a Radha, we need to first submit ourselves to another man. And although we may accept another man, we actually belong to Krishna. The man "marrying" a Radha also knows this. A Radha's lover is Krishna. The guru told me that unless we live as husband and wife, I will not be able to experience the love of Krishna. Hence we did so.'

'Did he actually marry you?' I asked.

'No,' she said. 'As he was a *sanyasi*, he was not allowed to marry anyone. But he fulfilled all the roles of a husband for me.'

'Is the guru still with you?'

'No. It has been several years since he attained samadhi. But Krishna is our permanent refuge. That love never ends. He is always with me. Truth be told, I feel the guru was but a tool to my realization of Krishna. He fulfilled his mission and left. I believe he would have attained heaven.' Pooja's face beamed as she said this.

We met Swami Vinaykraj the next day, who we thought could explain to us the exploitation of Radhas in Vrindavan better than anyone else. He had been in Vrindavan for more than two and a half decades. When I called him on the phone that morning, I told him we were interested in getting an overall picture of Vrindavan. When he heard where we were staying, he asked us to come to an ashram that was close by at 11 a.m.

Swami arrived at the appointed time. He was six feet tall, wore a long kurta and dhoti and sported a long beard along with long hair. Half of his beard had turned white. A plastic bag was all that he carried. He told us we could go to a house nearby where all the Swamis from the neighbouring ISKCON temple stayed to talk.

We got into the same autorickshaw as the previous day, whom we had paid five rupees per person as fare. However, when we alighted at the spot that Swami specified, the driver asked for fifteen rupees. Swami gave him ten rupees and told us to walk ahead. The driver persisted on the fare, but the Swami ignored him. We offered to clear the remaining fare, but Swami discouraged us and told us to keep moving. The driver then shouted something, at which Swami retorted without flinching, '*Jaa, ma choot* (Get lost, motherfucker).' Not just the driver, we were also stunned by Swami's use of expletives. He had dispelled the notion that men of god had to practise austerity in speech. Perhaps he sensed our shock, for he was silent the rest of the walk.

The Yamuna Bachao Abhiyan movement had been fighting for the protection of the Yamuna River under the leadership of Swami Jayakrishna Das. It was to his room that Swami Vinaykraj took us and began to expound on Vrindavan's curious social structure based on his experience.

'Women come to Vrindavan every day. However many there are, Vrindavan can accommodate them all. The ashrams have the space. The ashrams teach how to meditate about Krishna. This meditation can take different forms – peaceful, friendly, affectionate as in a parent–child relationship, loving as in a man–woman relationship, and many more. Of these, the man–woman relationship is given importance in Vrindavan. Some women here might have always been devotees of Krishna and would be familiar with the various methods of *upasana*. The mutts are meant for those who do not know. Everyone gets a chance to sing in the mornings and evenings, and they are rewarded for that. The mutts get huge donations from the pilgrims; hence, they do not begrudge the Radhas the payment for bhajans.'

'Does Vrindavan have the capacity to equitably accommodate all who come here?' I enquired.

'We have thought much about the income inequalities here. Anyway, we can't hope for great prosperity in Vrindavan because Lakshmi, the goddess of wealth, is not allowed to enter. Don't be surprised if you don't see much wealth here. There are so many temples in Vrindavan, but you won't find a single idol of Lakshmi. We have restricted her to the other side of the Yamuna.'

I recalled the mythological story of the goddess Lakshmi who left Vaikuntha and came to Vrindavan, fascinated by the Ras Lila of Krishna and Radha, but was denied entry. It was said that only those who submit to another can renounce the ego and only such persons can experience the love of Krishna. I made a case for Lakshmi: 'The reason Lakshmi was barred from Vrindavan was that she did not obey the instructions to be the loved one of someone in Vrindavan before loving Krishna. Is this obstinacy justified?'

'Sri Krishna spent 11 years of his life in Vrindavan. Legend has it that one night he started playing the flute and even the women who were breastfeeding their babies left them behind in search of him. When Krishna told the women their husbands would be looking for them, they said they did not want to live their lives depending on their husbands, who would anyway take care of them only till they died, but Krishna's love and protection was permanent. That was what they desired. The men who "marry" the women here know that Krishna is the lord of their minds, so the question of morals and values does not arise. Moreover, husbands also take pride in the fact that their wives worship Krishna. In all the homes here, everyone eats only after offering food to Krishna. Just as the wife takes care of her husband, she takes care of Krishna too. Krishna doesn't have separate vessels here, as would be the case when you serve a god. He is treated as a family member, and thus there are no such formalities. The truth is that the husbands of Vrindavan take pride in this.'

'Don't you think the husbands don't have any other choice?'

'No. Most homes here have a separate room for the husbands to sleep in. In smaller houses, a cot is kept outside. The husbands ensure their sex lives are only focused towards procreation.'

I remembered seeing the cots placed outside homes when we touched down in Vrindavan.

As Swami Jayakrishna Das had to go visit the demonstration platform of the Yamuna Bachao Abhiyan, we too decided to leave with him. As per his request to visit the marquee, we accompanied him in a car that he had arranged for. We continued our conversation with Swami Vinaykraj in the car.

Vinaykraj believed that Vrindavan took its current shape around 530 years ago, during Chaitanya Mahaprabhu's lifetime. His hometown was Mayapur, in the district of Nadia in Bengal. But he came to Vrindavan with the sole intent of reinstating the *nama sankeertanam* or the chanting of Krishna's names. In those days, when sati was practised, Chaitanya Prabhu offered a refuge to the women who wanted to escape death. I wondered whether he had also calculated that they would be useful for his proselytizing mission and brought the widows who followed him here to Vrindavan. The widows must have seen that as an escape from the horrible practice of sati. And although sati was banned by law, it didn't reflect in the attitude of the people. That is probably why widows had always tried to escape.

When I suggested that the Nadia widows must be coming to Vrindavan using the same route as 530 years ago, Swami Vinaykraj readily agreed. He admitted that after the death of Chaitanya Mahaprabhu, women could have been exploited in some of the ashrams. He had also heard stories. But he thought it was not possible any more. According to him, the establishment of the Gaudiya Mutt by Bhakti Siddhant Saraswati Thakur made a great difference in this regard. Some ashrams focused on the aspect of romantic love with the divine, and several had exploited the widows thus, including the heads of several mutts. The disciples of Bhakti Siddhant Saraswati, such as Swami Maharaj and Bhakti Vedant Swami, had put an end to such exploitation, he said.

'Can you say with absolute conviction such exploitative practices no longer occur in any ashrams now?' I asked him point-blank.

'Isolated incidents may occur but not to the extent that you imagine. Tell me, where can you escape those?' He caught me off guard with a question to which he clearly did not expect an answer.

Satish had told us about Dr Shivesh, who had devoted his life to improving the condition of the Radhas. When we arrived at his apartment, the doctor was alone. We introduced ourselves as journalists from Kerala. He began the conversation by saying the plight of the Radhas was pathetic and things had improved because of his work. I got a sense of what was about to come. The doctor was frustrated that his work was going unnoticed. He handed me several albums that had pictures of the doctor conducting medical camps among the Radhas. The pictures had been clicked in aesthetic poses, showing the good doctor examining his patients from several angles. It was no surprise that he had a towering presence in every picture. He pointed to a quote that had been put up on the wall and said that he lived by those words. Ironically, they read, 'Talk less, talk softly, talk sweetly'.

The doctor believed Indians were usually slow to appreciate things that were good for them, but foreigners weren't like that. He declared he had been receiving foreign donations that supported his initiatives. His family was in Kanpur, but he did not want to discuss them. Instead, he repeated he had come to Vrindavan as per Krishna's instructions to work for the welfare of his Radhas.

Since we were not going to get anything out of him other than stories of self-aggrandizement, we prepared to leave. Then he became particular that we should record our visit. He had no issues being featured in Malayalam newspapers and asked us to click pictures for the same. He proceeded to act out several poses, such as sitting in the driver's seat in the ambulance and such. We controlled our laughter with great difficulty and indulged him before bidding him goodbye.

We had also heard the name of a Dr Lakshmi who worked for the women in Vrindavan. I was not very hopeful about her either. She lived in a slum, among several huts. Though her house wasn't big, it was the only one in the neighbourhood with a concrete roof. We were received warmly, and the doctor, a middle-aged lady, introduced the two-year-old child she was playing with in the veranda as her grandchild. The child seemed to resent our hijacking of her grandmother and looked at us with disdain.

Though she was slow to open up at first, the doctor exploded with fury when we asked her about the NGOs that maintained the ashrams. She believed most of the NGOs here existed only to embezzle the benefits the widows were supposed to receive. 'They do not get their rations, but the NGOs clear out entire ration shops in their name. Radhas do not have a clear idea about their rights. If anyone tries to ask them, the NGOs threaten them into silence. There are several government schemes that provide money to the Radhas, but they are never properly disbursed. The NGOs might be receiving the money, but how can you call it social work? There are people who even embezzle the money meant for buying chappals and sheets. Bank accounts are opened to transfer money to the Radhas. These NGOs get the withdrawal forms signed in advance from the Radhas under their control. And once the Radhas die, they use these forms to siphon off the money. There have been several cases where NGOs have not informed the banks about the Radhas' deaths and have continued to misappropriate the money.

'When a Radha dies, the NGO gets up to ₹3,000 to cremate her. But until recently, they would tie up the body in a sack and throw it into the Yamuna. Any ornaments on the Radha would be stolen. Now that the Supreme Court has finally interfered, there are some changes. Still, it cannot be said that Vrindavan is totally clean.'

'Does it create economic disparity when so many women come here together?' I asked.

'If you go to Nadia, you will see many of them wandering

around, trying to find buses to Vrindavan. Almost a hundred of them come here every day. Although they claim it is their devotion to Krishna that brought them here, most of them come here to mitigate their hunger.'

'But aren't the NGOs doing good work too?' I probed.

'There may be a handful. But most focus on getting money from abroad into their accounts.'

'How did you get into this field?' we asked.

Dr Lakshmi pondered over the question. She slowly began, 'Four years ago, I married off my daughter. The groom was from Jaipur, Rajasthan. When my daughter became pregnant, both her husband's family and our family were ecstatic. After the first scan, however, it became clear that the baby would be a girl, and their attitude began to change. They kept her at a distance. By the time the second scan confirmed it was a girl, they left her here. That was a big shock. I continued to believe everything would be fine once the baby was born. I was delighted when my daughter gave birth to a healthy, beautiful girl child. I was confident her father would give up his pettiness and come and visit his baby. But that hope was in vain. Even in the midst of all the happiness this little angel gave us, this fact continued to burn me from the inside. Later, as I talked to others, I began to understand that people who think that girls are a curse have their own justifications and fears. Beyond social and economic evils such as dowry, they mix up superstitions with their justifications. That makes them forget everything else – their love for their children, compassion, duty etc. The curse of being a girl overshadows any of those. So I gave up the hope that her father would come for her, and it is no longer a problem for me.'

The doctor paused for a minute to regain her composure as she wiped her eyes. I remained silent. Then she started again, 'I have thought a lot about why girls are so discriminated against in our country. They face humiliation and discrimination at every point in their lives – as a foetus, as babies, as children, as young women and as widows. I felt that I should study more about the lives of such women. That is how I decided to learn more about the widows of Vrindavan who are the discards of our society. Today, I have my daughter and granddaughter with me. I do not ignore them and can never do so. Nor can I ignore the women who come to Vrindavan.' She began to cry again.

The two-year-old child had, by then, grown bored of playing alone and walked inside in search of her grandmother. She climbed on her lap. Though her cuteness tempted us to pinch her cheeks, the look of aversion she had on her face stopped us.

We met two teachers during our visit to a school in Vrindavan. Notably, this place stood out for featuring Christian symbols, making it unique from all other institutions in Vrindavan. But it did not have the grandeur and dignity of those run by Christian missionaries in Andhra Pradesh, and even the teachers spoke disappointedly.

They told us it had been months since they were paid.

It seemed to me that religious conversion was not as prevalent here as it was in Andhra. There were only nine Christian families in the panchayat, they said, grumbling that Hindus had all the money. 'All the banks have branches here. Have you seen so many branches in any panchayat? All those who visit this place donate generously to the Mutts.'

'Is prostitution rampant here?' I asked them.

'Is anything unavailable in Vrindavan? Drugs, women, fish, meat... everything is available but in secret. If you stay here for six months, you will know.'

I was curious to know if there was any truth in the allegations beyond their frustrations. So I asked our rickshaw puller whether women were available in Vrindavan.

'All that has stopped in Vrindavan now, sir,' he replied.

'Were they available earlier?'

'In plenty. All the ashrams conducted that business. The people who visited here would use those women.'

'Don't you think it will still be practised to some extent?'

'That may be possible. But if so, the women won't be available to strangers. You need to have influence inside the ashrams.'

'Why do these women need to beg then?'

'Well, not everyone gets the business, sir. Take a look yourself. How many women come to Vrindavan every day? Do you see enough men?' The puller turned around to assess our response. Pramod and I started conversing in Malayalam while the puller continued to pedal silently. Then he asked us, 'Saab, do you want a woman?'

We looked at each other. Were we going to get a peek into one of the ashrams that indulged in prostitution? I eagerly answered, 'Yes, that would be good.'

'You can come home with me and use my wife. Just pay me 200 rupees.' We were too stunned to say anything.

'You won't find lower rates in any ashram, sir,' he reiterated to remove any misgivings that we may have had, and turned to face us and gauge our response.

I felt as if time had frozen under the weight of his words and that the rickshaw no longer moved forward. Finally, after what seemed like a long time, we reached our destination. Both of us jumped out quickly. Though we had hired the rickshaw for 20 rupees, we gave him a 50-rupee note and asked him to buy sweets for his children. Maybe that gave him the impression that we were rich, because he repeated his earlier offer: 'Saab, you can come home and sleep with my wife.'

# 11

# The Entombed Lives of Kamathipura

MY NEXT DESTINATION WAS MUMBAI'S INFAMOUS Kamathipura. I had decided to visit Kamathipura right when I came to know that many devadasis from Karnataka end up there. Although smaller than Sonagachi, Kamathipura occupies a prominent place among India's red-light areas. In the southern parts of the country, a 'red-light street' is immediately associated with Kamathipura, probably because of the stories carried home by young men who migrate to Mumbai for employment. We had also been told that devadasis from Karnataka eventually end up in Kamathipura as well.

Since Pramod was unable to accompany me, I was travelling alone this time. The Diwali celebrations hadn't quite ended on the day I reached Mumbai. The city has numerous tales of cultural heritage and history to relate, but its hectic pace drowns everything else. Everyone seems to be in a tearing hurry. During my journey from Vashi station to the Chhatrapati Shivaji Maharaj Terminal (CSMT), I made friends with an American named Steve Walk, an IT professional from the US who had come to holiday in India. He asked me why Indians were always in a hurry after he saw the crowds run towards a half-empty train. 'I see this rush in trains, buses and on the roads. But the best part is that even when you are boarding a plane, where your seat is guaranteed once you check in, Indians are in a hurry.' There were examples all over Mumbai to prove him right. When we reached India's busiest station, CSMT, I too hurried up to get a cab for the next part of my journey. It was getting dark, and I had to reach Kamathipura as soon as possible. Only if I got there before the regular work hours of the women began would I be able to find someone to talk to.

I alighted from the taxi in front of Maharashtra College. A narrow lane across from the college led to Kamathipura, with other smaller lanes branching out from it, imaginatively called First Lane, Second Lane etc. Traders squatted on both sides, and if I thought Sonagachi was crowded, there were more than twice the number of roadside shops here. In Sonagachi, only its residents patronized these stores, but here, everyone seemed to be a customer.

There weren't too many women out on the streets. One could see tiny, stuffy rooms here and there. One or two women sat outside on stools. I ignored them and walked about 300 metres ahead, where I came to another bifurcation and more lanes and paths. I walked through the entire network of interconnected lanes and finally came back to the main road. I was surprised. Not a single agent had approached me! I walked inside one of the hotels on the main road and called for tea.

'Do you need anything other than tea, sir?' the boy asked me.

'No,' I replied quickly.

He returned with the tea. As I finished drinking it, another man approached me and asked pointedly, 'Is tea all that you want?'

I shook my head to convey my position again.

'If you want something from outside the shop, you can order that too,' he said with a laugh. I returned the laugh. When I came out, the men who had gathered outside said something looking at me. I ignored them and walked ahead. It had started getting dark, but the street lights and the shops kept the area well illuminated. I could see women leaning on the yellow-and-black taxis parked on the roadside. They were dressed in saris, and most of them looked above 40. A few looked to be younger and wore mostly jeans and T-shirts. And while I could only see one or two women sitting outside the cramped rooms earlier, small groups now sat outside. The rooms beyond them were also filled with women – not really women but young girls.

The taxi drivers and roadside traders were trying to finish off their remaining fireworks, looking for a place where they could ignite those fireworks that burst into colours in the sky. The women leaning on the cabs gave them suggestions while also warning them to be careful. Some of the men tried to impress them, bragging about their firecrackers.

As I walked by, an old man leaning on a taxi, probably the driver himself, muttered under his breath, 'Pretty girls are available.' He artfully laid the bait by repeating this in three south Indian languages, rightly guessing that I was from the south. I turned around, and he approached me instantly. He repeated the sales pitch in the three languages. When I told him I was from Kerala, he tried to tempt me by offering 'Kerala girls' too.

I took him aside and told him, 'It's not what you think... I have come with a different purpose. I have come from Kerala to study about the problems of women here.'

The man looked disappointed at not getting any business and couldn't contain his anger. His voice toughened. 'There are no problems here. Please do not try to create problems where there are none. You can have the deal if you want. I have "stock" ranging from 200 to 2,000.'

Things would not work out for me if I went down this line, so I changed tack. 'I would like to see a dance. Is that possible here?'

'There are girls who dance like you have never seen

before. There are women who do *mujra*. Do you want them?' he asked.

All I knew about *mujra* was limited to the books I had read, where the dance was depicted as a vestige of India's Islamic past. In *mujra*, women dance to the pace of *ghazals*, and its movements are quite similar to kathak. I decided to use it as my calling card.

'An ordinary *mujra* is available for 500, but the good ones can cost you up to 5,000,' the man began to negotiate.

'I will decide after I see the girls,' I said.

The old man asked me to follow him. He turned into a by-lane and climbed the narrow stairs of an old building. When we reached our destination, he removed his shoes before entering and asked me to do the same. We then walked into a veranda, where six to seven middle-aged women sat. Beyond that was a big hall, almost 20 by 15 feet in size. Long wooden cots sat in the corners. Each cot had a cupboard that acted as a divider. There was some space between each cot, maybe for visitors to walk. Both sides had two big cupboards facing each other, thus keeping the beds out of view of each other. The big hall was divided into ten small rooms in this manner. Cabins had a door, which was kept open but curtained.

I looked at the women sitting outside. They smiled at me as per the courtesy extended to a customer. The taxi driver explained things to them in a language I couldn't follow.

'You want to see *mujra*?' one woman asked me in Hindi.

'Yes.'

The woman had been chewing paan for a while and spat it outside, anticipating a conversation full of bargaining. 'Good *mujras* will cost you from 5,000 to 6,000.'

'Is this the original *mujra*?' I pretended to be a picky customer.

'There is only one *mujra*. We are from Ujjain, renowned for the world's best *mujra* dancers. If you have the money, we will show you.'

I took out a 500-rupee note from my pocket. 'I don't want to see the *mujra*; I just want to hear about it.'

She exchanged looks with others. The taxi driver then intervened to facilitate things. 'Take the money, and tell him about the dance.'

'Hasn't this guy come to get hooked up?' she asked the broker.

'He sounded strange. I don't know,' he backtracked.

'Motherfucker,' the woman abused him.

Hearing this, the broker asked me to get up. He shoved his hands into my pockets and emptied them. Thankfully I had not brought my camera with me. Once again I was being searched as thoroughly as someone who had come to negotiate terms at a terrorist camp.

The driver took out my phone and whatever cash I had and showed it to the woman. 'Mobile,' he announced, as if to placate her.

She grew calmer after realizing I did not have a camera

or a recorder. 'Why do you want to learn about the dance?' she now enquired.

'I want to know about the dance as well as your hometown.'

'Hometown? This is my hometown now. And I cannot talk about this place, so don't expect anything of that sort.' Her tone hardly concealed her anger.

The broker had lost his patience by now. He stretched out his hands, asking for his share. I gave him a hundred rupees, which he touched to his eyes and left happily. The woman put the 500 I gave her into her blouse. From their conversation with the broker, I had figured out her name was Meena.

'Your hometown is Ujjain, right? I want to know more about it,' I slowly asked her again.

'It used to be Ujjain. Not any more.'

'They drove us out of there,' one of Meena's companions, who wore a yellow sari, interjected.

Meena abused her for talking in between, asking her why she had to butt in.

Two men walked in at that point, another broker and a customer who looked to be about 45. The broker weaved through us and took the customer to the hall with the cabins. He seemed to be a regular, going by how at ease he looked. They spoke for a bit, then the broker walked out and handed Meena a few notes. 'I have taken my 50,' he said.

Meena turned to the woman in the yellow sari and gestured to her. The woman got up and went inside. She drew the curtains of one of the cabins and asked the customer to step inside. Then she took two condoms from the table next to where we sat. My eyes followed her instinctively, and Meena didn't like it one bit. 'Have you come here to see a dance or to see how other people do it?' she asked sarcastically.

'But you are not telling me anything about the dance,' I countered.

She was quiet for some time, perhaps weighing how much she should tell me. Then she began, 'Have you heard of servants of the temple? That is what we were – devadasis. Now we have become like this.'

I was stunned! I had wondered how I would find devadasis among the thousands of women in these streets. I hadn't found a devadasi girl even after visiting Sonagachi three times over. And now, all of a sudden, it seemed these women were waiting for me.

I kept my surprise under wraps and didn't let out anything. She continued, 'There were a lot of devadasis in Ujjain. Girls are given off to the temples. Our mothers were also devadasis. Devadasis are not supposed to have children. If they do, it is believed that god is angry with them. So they have no choice but to make their children devadasis as well. Others are sent to become devadasis due to other reasons. Look at Remya here. Her parents could not bring her up because of poverty. So they gave her to the temple as a devadasi.'

'How did you learn *mujra* as a devadasi?' I asked.

Before she could reply, I saw the customer's pants fall out of the bed and onto the floor in the cabin inside. I noticed it by chance. Meena followed my gaze and saw it too. She couldn't help laughing. I got emboldened too and broke into the laugh I had been stifling for a while.

Meena abruptly stopped laughing and spoke seriously. Her history was the same as that of the devadasis attached to temples in south India. I asked her again, 'Where did you learn *mujra*?'

'We had some Muslim neighbours in Pinjarvadi. They knew *mujra* and taught us. In those days, if we wanted to keep our customers happy, we had to know everything. A madam called Suneeta took care of things. Without someone like her, we wouldn't have been able to do things for ourselves. Everyone would cheat us otherwise. Suneeta insisted that we learn *mujra* as the people who came to watch *mujra*, who were predominantly Muslim businessmen, shelled out a lot of money. Everyone wanted to see fresh faces dance. They wanted to sleep with them after the dance too, and that would bring in more money. Suneeta would see to it that there was a regular supply of new girls.'

The woman and her customer emerged from the cabin, settling their clothes. He cracked a lewd joke before leaving. The woman joined us.

'When you say new girls, were those also devadasis?' I returned to our conversation.

'Girls from famished families – and some happen to be devadasis. When the parents could not bring them up any more, they would give them to us. Sometimes, Suneeta went to their homes and picked up the girls. People would flock to see younger girls dance. In those days, we didn't lack customers. Because we had young girls, loyal customers would keep returning. We could charge any amount of money for these girls. And since the money came through the girls, Suneeta made sure the girls had all sorts of comforts. Initially, a new girl would bed only one customer. When he had had enough, she would be given to another. After that, she was open for anybody. That was the usual procedure. Everything was controlled by Suneeta. The zamindars used to call her the queen of Ujjain.'

'Did you leave Ujjain in hopes of finding something better?' I asked.

'Who left Ujjain? We were shunted out of there, don't you know?' The woman wearing the yellow sari repeated.

Meena did not abuse her this time, no longer irritated at her interruption.

The woman began to tell her story. 'Do you remember the Maha Kumbh Mela in Ujjain? That was 10 years ago. The ruling government was worried that *sanyasis* who came for the Kumbh would be distracted and destroyed by devadasis and expelled us. They did give us time to leave, but we didn't. Where can we go leaving home? Finally, when the stipulated time ran out, the police came and beat us up, forcing us to leave. We literally ran for our lives. Some of us went to Nagpur. Others came here.'

Meena interjected, 'Suneeta herself told us there is a red-light area called Kamathipura in Mumbai and asked us to board a train to this place. About 500 of us took the train to Mumbai that day. Suneeta told us she would call us back once everything was settled. But she did not come here. We hear the government is still strict about keeping Ujjain clean of prostitutes. So we might not be able to work even if we go back. We had a lot of money saved up there. Maybe Suneeta took all of it. Well, it was money gathered by selling young girls, so let her keep it.'

By then, another customer came in, led by the same broker who brought me. The man looked to be hardly 25. 'He has only 200. Someone please go with him,' the broker requested.

Meena once again abused him. She gestured to the oldest woman in the group to go with the boy. The woman said something in the negative, so Meena turned to the woman in the yellow sari once more. She got up, took the condoms and went inside with the boy. The broker smiled at me, gave Meena a few notes, probably from the new customer, and left. The yellow-sari woman demanded a hundred rupees as rent for the room from the boy, to which he replied he didn't have any money. She quickly searched his pockets and his wallet and pocketed a hundred rupees and some change he had stashed somewhere.

'That is for me to go back home in the cab!' the boy protested.

'Take the bus,' she said and gave him back the change.

'You can keep the change,' he said. 'I want the 100. I do not know this place enough to use the bus.'

We then heard a litany of abuses before the woman gave him a 50. 'That's enough for the taxi.'

The boy resigned himself to accept whatever came his way. The woman drew the curtain and stepped inside. The boy followed. The women outside cracked jokes in a language I could not understand and laughed. I laughed along nonetheless.

Before the laughter had died down, the broker brought in another customer. Meena dropped her air of friendliness and told me, 'You need to leave now. This is the peak time for customers. Come back during the day.'

I left before she fixed the next proposal. I thought it would be dangerous to return by the same lane, so I took another route out. Men continued to light up crackers here too. The fireworks scattered myriad colours in the sky. Although the women watched the show and laughed in delight, their eyes scoured the road for customers, as did their brokers.

Before long, a broker came in front of me. 'Madras?' he asked.

'Yes.'

He continued on his prepared script. 'Do you want beautiful girls who look like film stars, sir?'

'How much?'

'Five hundred.'

I gave him 500 and told him, 'I have come here to do a project on devadasis. I want to meet devadasis from Karnataka.'

He looked at me carefully. I grew worried. Before I could decipher what he was thinking, he emptied out my pockets and examined the contents. A couple of other cab drivers walked towards us. I felt my fear double. I had never ventured into such areas alone so far. I wondered whether that decision would cost me dear.

The drivers asked the broker if there was a problem. He said no and sent them off. I could finally breathe normally again. He took me to the side of the road and asked gravely, 'Is this for Madras University?'

'Yes,' I too replied with equal gravity.

'There were a lot of such girls here, sir. Some got rescued. Now there is only one. She might have been a devadasi. Let us go and check for ourselves.'

As usual, we walked inside a building through a dingy and cramped staircase. There were a group of women here too, with one girl who wore jeans and a top. He called her inside, and she came in with condoms. The broker told me I could ask her questions only in his presence. I agreed to his terms. He gave her a brief introduction of what I wanted. The girl told me her story on the condition that she would not be named.

'I was born in a village called Saundatti in Karnataka. My mother was a jogamma. I don't know who my father is. My mother doesn't either. My mother had vowed she would make me a servant to Yellamma when I turned 11. But the police did not allow her to do so. That is when an uncle known to my mother brought me here. I was made to stay at a baba's house, where men would come in the evening. Several days later, the police came with guns and took me and four other girls. Baba was arrested, and us girls were put in a hostel. After a court case, Baba ended up in jail. We were put up in the hostel at government expense till we were 18. After that, I returned home. But no one was willing to take me in. I couldn't work, as no one would hire a jogamma. The belief is that if a jogamma works somewhere, that house will be destroyed. So I returned to Mumbai. Now I am here, I get meals three times a day, and once in five or six months, I go see my mother. The saab here who runs the brothel gives me some money then, and I give it to my mother.'

The girl was 21. She said that several girls who were rescued along with her by the police had come back. Some of them took up other work. She mentioned a girl called Soumya and gave me her number. She instructed me not to reveal under any circumstances that she had given me the number. I agreed. Though I had more questions, she wasn't ready to speak more.

As the broker and I were leaving, we saw a young man about 30 years old standing with the other women and another broker. The young man, who was Tamil, had gone with a woman who took all his money and sent him off. All that remained was 200 rupees, which he had carefully hidden in his shirt. He wanted to get the job done within that. That's why he was here, the broker explained.

'Did you go with one of the women on the road?' a woman asked, which the broker translated into Tamil.

The customer nodded.

'They are plain prostitutes. Women with dignity won't step out on the road. Look at us. You can see us only if you come here. If you go to prostitutes, they will rob you. What did you expect?' the woman ranted in Hindi. The customer didn't seem to care; he wanted the job done, not listen to a lecture on morals.

I left the place pondering over the difference between prostitutes and dignified women.

Soumya worked at a call centre at Santa Cruz. I went there to meet her. When I told her I was conducting a survey on girls who had escaped from Kamathipura and were now leading a better life, the first thing she asked me was how

I got her number. I told her the police gave it to me, after which she did not ask me any further questions. As she was in a hurry to get back to work, she told me her story quickly.

Soumya was also from Karnataka. When she was studying in grade 11, aged 17, she fell in love with a cab driver, but she didn't know his background. 'I was really brainless at the time.' She lowered her head, probably in guilt. 'I boarded a train with him to Mumbai one day, my first visit. He asked me to stay in a house which had some older girls too. He told me it was a friend's house. But on the second day, he took my earrings and chain and said he was going to the bank. After that, the other girls brought me to Kamathipura and told me to sit in a room with several other women. I cried, saying I wanted to see the man. They laughed at that and said the saab of that house had bought me off the man. I did not realize what was happening. I just wanted to see my parents. There was no one to help me, and I broke down mentally. I told them my parents would pay them any sum if they let me go. They advised me to talk to the saab. When I met him, he laughed cruelly at my request and said that he would take me home after making the most of me and take money from them too.' Soumya went pale at the recollection. She continued, 'One day, they bathed me with turmeric and other powders. I sat around for three days after that, doing nothing. In the evening, some man or the other would come. One of the older girls would go with them inside and come back later. I couldn't understand anything. Four or five days later, the owner asked me to go inside. The man looked to be at least 40. He asked me to remove my clothes. I was terrified and couldn't move. As he approached me, I got more and more scared.

'My mind was blurred with a dreamlike vision – of him feeling sorry for me and leaving while my mother came and hugged me. But that was obviously a dream. Reality was nothing like that. He assaulted me. One year was spent like that, with countless people doing the same thing day after day.

'One day, the police walked in, accompanied by a few other people, and rescued me and four other girls. After that, I stayed in the government hostel till I was 18 and studied. Once I left the place, I tried for several jobs. I finally got this one, and now I am settled here.'

'Are you terrified of your past?' I asked.

'No. I never think about the past,' she answered abruptly, as if she had pre-empted my question.

'Why doesn't the police rescue all the women in Kamathipura?'

'I don't know. There are several who have gone back to the job after being rescued. One girl who was rescued with me is back there now. She says it is because she cannot get any other job. It might be true.'

I don't know if Soumya was telling the truth when she

said it was time for her to get back to work. Maybe she was just trying to escape from me and my distressing questions.

I wanted to find out who had been responsible for the rescue operations and was introduced to Anson Thomas by the Mumbai photographer of the *Malayala Manorama*, RS Gopan.

Originally from Pathanamthitta, Kerala, Anson had been living in Mumbai for many years and recounted his stories on the way to his residence. He had rescued more than 750 girls, but unlike many of the people I had met on my travels so far, he was not interested in parading his achievements. All he had to talk about was the indifference and non-cooperation of the police and the government. To sum it up, he was in deep despair.

Anson, who was a customs officer during 1989–2010, started rescuing girls in Kamathipura towards the early 1990s. 'It is only after you visit the police station five times that they will agree to accompany you for a rescue. We would have otherwise rescued at least five times the number of girls till now. The local police is just not interested. That is a major problem.'

'How do girls come into this world?' I asked.

'In many ways. There are those who are promised jobs in Mumbai by agents. Then there are the naïve ones who follow their lovers, and women even sold by their own husbands!'

'How does a rescue operation happen?'

'The rescue operations are mostly meant to rescue underage girls. We first identify where such girls are being housed. There are some people among them who help us – pimps, agents and others. Once they pass on the details, I pose as a customer and go to the place – but I cannot do that any more as they know me by now. So nowadays I send someone who's trustworthy, and once they confirm the report and come back with the girls' details, if possible, we go to the police. We visit the brothel once more, after which the police secure it and rescue the girls. But things are not so easy most of the times. Like I said, the police agree to accompany us for a rescue only after we make at least five visits to the police station.

'Then the next challenge is in the court. Very often the girls change their statements out of fear. A prolonged legal battle is required to put even one trafficker behind bars. Now I am on all of their hit lists.'

'Is there any point in rescuing the girls if they cannot find other means to sustain themselves?' I meant to play the devil's advocate, but my question infuriated Anson.

'Would we push our mothers or sisters to the streets to prostitute? It is easy to find justifications. If Indians have taken the pledge that all Indians are their brothers and sisters, I would say it is an insult to that pledge to stay silent when their sisters are reduced to waiting on the streets for random men. When the Nirbhaya rape case happened in Delhi, there were many painted faces who appeared on TV and exploded in anger. But there are a 1,000 "Nirbhayas" being raped here every single day. None of them has a problem with that. And what about the organizations founded to protect the girls? They are busy conducting seminars and discussions in five-star hotels on whether to call them prostitutes or sex workers. They don't want to solve anything at the ground level. Several years ago, I was called to Kerala by an organization. At the meeting, we were debating a resolution to ensure sex workers did not get too low a wage and were getting at least 100 rupees per client. I asked them to imagine women from their own houses selling their bodies. Would they then discuss their rates? I don't know if the resolution got passed.'

'What is the solution then?' I asked, in an effort to placate him.

'Each one of us should feel genuine pain. Just imagine how terrible the torture and abuse experienced by the children inside these red-light areas must be! It's only then that you can sincerely do anything for them. Take, for example, the case of Vijaya, the girl I rescued a few years ago. Today, she is fighting for other girls who come out of Kamathipura. Her work is absolutely genuine because she has experienced first-hand the brutalities inside that place.'

I learnt that Vijaya was currently a volunteer with the Nav Jeevan organization run by the Marthoma Sabha in Murbad, 75 kilometres away from Kalyan, on the outskirts of Mumbai. Nav Jeevan focuses on rehabilitating the children of sex workers by providing them with an education. I first went to their office in Mumbai and got the permission to meet Vijaya. The priests in charge of Nav Jeevan arranged for me to travel to Murbad in the same bus that was carrying the teachers.

It was peak noon when we arrived. The teachers asked me to sit in the office and got busy. All the staff at the organization were from Kerala, so when they heard I had come, they came by and spoke to me. I wondered if any of them could be Vijaya. A little while later, a person who had walked past me earlier approached me. She introduced herself as Vijaya.

She pulled up a chair and told me that the priests had explained why I had come. She said she had been interviewed on TV once, while several papers had also featured her story. Maybe it was because of that, she gave precise bits of information as she recounted her story.

'I come from Cuddalore, near Chennai. My father's

name was Ahmed Hamza, and my mother was Fatima Zaara. My original name was Nadia Bi. We used to live in a rented house and suffered unspeakable poverty. My mother would get a horrible stomach pain every now and then. On most days, we could afford only one meal. One day, my father gave us 20 rupees and told my mother and me to go buy rice from the neighbourhood shop. When we were on our way back, someone ran up to my mother and told her my father had hung himself.

'My mother ran home, dragging me by one hand and holding the rice bag dearly to her chest with the other. Unlike in the movies, she could not afford to fling the bag.' Vijaya couldn't help but smile at her dark humour. She continued with that same wry smile, 'I don't know if you would understand, sir. We faced dire poverty.' She paused for a bit. I didn't utter a word.

She seemed to be thinking about where to pick up the thread of the story now. Then, as if she had rearranged her memories, she said, 'There was a belief that houses where suicides happen are cursed. Some people got together and burnt down our small house. For the next few days, my mother and I spent our days in the mosque's veranda. But the people in charge there asked us to leave soon. So we went to my father's relative. I was 11 then. One day, when my mother had gone out somewhere, someone drugged me and smuggled me off in a vehicle. When I regained consciousness, I was in another house, but I didn't know where I was. When I cried, saying I wanted to see my mother, some women comforted me by saying they would bring her soon. Two days later, I was moved to another house where the women had red lips and wore deep-cut blouses. It was a scary atmosphere. A *hijada* wielded supreme control there.'

I got a sense that Vijaya didn't have to struggle to remember her past. It lived inside her and had become a part of her. 'The day after I reached, I was bathed with oil and turmeric in a big function. There were a lot of pujas. I did not understand anything. I thought I would be able to see my mother after the puja was over. But what unfolded that night was something I could never have imagined. A man came in, and the *hijada* told me to go into the room with him and make him happy. I went inside. When the man closed the door and walked towards me, I screamed in fear. He tried to subdue me. I fought him back. So he went out and created a scene, saying he was being beaten up by girls after parting with all his money. The *hijada* trembled in anger and strode inside the room. Before I could say anything, he slapped me across the face, flinging me on the ground. He picked me up and tossed me on the next bed. He tied my hands up with a shawl and my legs with a rope. Then he went out, hurling choicest abuses all the while, after which he sent in the man again. This time, he assaulted me with renewed anger as I lay there, tied up helplessly.

'I was trapped with that *hijada* for three years. Then the police came with Anson *anna*, secured the area and captured all the *hijadas*. When Anson *anna* asked me to come out, I ran in terrified. I thought it was one of the men who came there every day to assault me. But Anson *anna* told me not to be scared and comforted me. That's when I felt confident enough to step out of there. I was put in the government hostel and started going to school. When I turned 18, I went home to see my mother. But I couldn't find her. Everyone told me that she had died. But I cannot believe that, and I keep praying to this day she is alive.

'I didn't want to stay in the village. I came back to Mumbai and did odd jobs here and there. Then Anson *anna* asked me to talk to the other girls who had been rescued. Most of the time, girls end up returning to the profession, mostly out of fear or because they cannot find other jobs. The girls will then give a testimony in court that favours the men who had put them up for sale and against those who rescued them. That's how traffickers escape the law's clutches, and Anson *anna* wanted me to counsel the girls and tell them about the life that awaited them once they escaped. When a person who was inside talks to them, the girls get more courage. I am currently counselling four rescued girls.'

'Why did you change your name?' I asked her.

'The *hijada* made me change it, saying Muslim names are not suitable in the business.' Vijaya smiled dryly. 'Do you know I once had beautiful, long hair. My mother would dress it up in all kinds of ways and show it off proudly to her relatives. She would be upset even if one strand came off. Then when I was trafficked, the older girls would fight for a chance to loosen my hair and tie it up again. The *hijada* would also say my hair was the Lakshmi of his brothel. "Your hair is your beauty. Let more people come in to see it. Untie your hair and stand there." If I didn't comply, he would abuse me and forcefully untie my hair.

'Then one day, a customer was so angry with me when I did not obey him that he grabbed me by the hair and crashed my face against a window.' Vijaya showed me the scar on her forehead. 'And though I began to bleed heavily, he continued to do what he wanted with my body.' Her eyes became wet at the recollection. 'So the first thing I did after I was rescued was to cut my hair.' Vijaya could no longer stop her tears. I grew numb at the wounds that the past had inflicted on her. Courage alone is not enough, I realized. You need to have a mind that is ready to cry too. Only then could we do something for those who suffered. Let Vijaya cry, I thought. In her tears, I tried to find the resilience and hope that would bring out several other girls from the miseries of fate.

# 12

# Saundatti's Full Moon

DEEP IN THE HEART OF BELGAUM IN KARNATAKA IS A TOWN called Saundatti, once the capital of the Ratta dynasty that ruled Belgaum until the 13th century and where the devadasi tradition ran very deep, especially at the famous Yellamma Gudda temple. During *Maghapournami*, a large number of devadasis visit the Yellamma temple in Saundatti, similar to the Uchangi temple in Davanagere. I knew I had to visit Saundatti during *Maghapournami*.

I arrived in Saundatti on the full moon of *Magha* in February 2014, locally known as the *Bharata honnima*. Two others – Mangalapuram visual media professional Pyarilal, and photojournalist Shaji Vettipuram – had accompanied me. The previous night, I had set up an appointment with Seethavva Jodatthi, executive officer of the Karnataka State Women Development Organization, at her office in Gattaprabha. This organization was very different from the Devadasi Liberation Front, with better networks. They ran their own school and seemed to manage things professionally. Seethavva didn't know who Renuka was, but her story was not very different from that of Renuka's. Both had been devadasis at one time.

Women belonging to the mather and kamble castes were normally turned into devadasis.

Seethavva belonged to the kamble caste and came from a family which had six children, and as per the instructions of the *gowda* (the landlord) of the village, she too was made a devadasi. Seethavva took us through what her organization did in the state. If a girl was not married off by the time she turned 18, members of the organization visited the house to check whether this was under the instruction of the *gowdas* in the community, who still held sway despite the ban on devadasis. The usual modus operandi was to conduct the devadasi rituals at home itself. Seethavva said her volunteers remained vigilant to ensure this does not happen.

'Is it good to insist girls should be married off by 18?' I asked her.

'Right and wrong are always relative based on the traditions of a particular area. If a girl is not married off by 18 here, there is always a chance that she may fall victim to another societal evil. That's why we need to remain vigilant. We do not insist the girls should be married off by 18, but we investigate the reasons why she is not. Personally, I believe we should marry girls off at a young age and make them secure,' Seethavva elaborated.

'Then why didn't you marry?'

'Who will want to marry me? I already have three children.'

She hadn't mentioned this earlier, so concealing my shock, I asked her, 'Won't the father of the children accept you?'

'Unfortunately, what happened in those times cannot be changed now,' she said in a resigned tone.

We left her a little after, but we couldn't go much further ahead because a colourful procession of decorated carts and people had crowded the road. Some of the carts hoisted flags in bright colours, while the heads and horns of the cattle that pulled the carts were also decorated with vermilion. Their bodies were covered with glitter powder in various colours. Some animals were tied up to the back of the cart as well. Our driver, Manoj, explained to us this was to switch the animals when the ones at the front got tired. We got out to take some pictures. Seeing our cameras, some of the cart drivers halted to speak to us. They were all going to Saundatti, and would reach by the next morning. There were women of all ages – small girls to old, ailing women – sitting on the carts. The younger girls watched us with great curiosity.

I was scared all these girls would be turned into devadasis. However, our driver said that since the ban had come into effect, people had stopped taking girls to the temple as all devadasi rituals were conducted at home now, so it was unlikely these children were being taken for the same. 'There may be some people who have promised the goddess that after doing the *dandaavathu*, they will take the girls home and make them devadasis. But it would be impossible to find out who they are,' he said. He tried his best to make us understand what *dandaavathu* meant, but he could not. He finally gave up, noting we would understand it as soon as we saw it at the temple.

Some groups were on their way back from the temple after the *darshan*. A long bridge stood over the river Malaprabha in a place called Gokak. We got off before the bridge to survey the surroundings. The river stretched out below us, and the afternoon sun blazed over our heads. Several carts had been parked on the vast riverbank, a resting spot for those visiting the Yellamma Gudda temple.

As we walked towards them, we saw that a majority of them were devadasis from their matted hair and their ornaments. When we introduced ourselves as journalists, some of them walked away. A few others, however, were eager to talk, with similar complaints as earlier – about not getting pensions and the like. The women who had walked away slowly returned. We saw that all of their hair was matted. They then told us that in the previous year at Saundatti, a government initiative had rounded up all the women who had matted hair and cut away the matted locks. They had avoided us fearing we had come for the same purpose. The women submitted their matted locks as proof that they were devadasis, which they considered as a blessing from the goddess. But several others had also faked such locks and pretended to be devadasis to have themselves registered as devadasis and secure the benefits. The government had taken necessary steps to counter this fraud. Officials undertook a proper count of devadasis and checked their details before confirming. They did not accept matted hair alone as proof to be counted as a devadasi.

The devadasis had nothing against all of this. But when the officials began to forcibly cut off their locks with the help of the police, they could not accept it. If the officials learnt someone was not a devadasi, all they needed to do was to deny them the pension. Why should they cut the hair which is the goddess's blessing? the devadasis asked. They were worried that such unsavoury incidents would be repeated this year, which was why several of them had stayed away from the temple.

We saw that several women had walked into the river and were conducting some rituals. When we asked them, they said they were on their way back from the temple. One of them held a rustic *veena* that was made out of metal strings stretched out on a block of wood. Two others held cymbals. Six granite stones, the size of a palm, had been placed on the riverbank. One of them applied vermilion on the stones. Another arranged puja items on a leaf in front of the stones. Once this was done, another started singing a eulogy for the goddess. The woman holding the *veena* strummed the song on the instrument and sang it loudly. When the song reached a crescendo, the woman started jumping in fervour. The others in the group tried to restrain her. Finally, she let out what seemed like a cry. Her face was devoid of any expression, but she continued to cry out loud in a steady rhythm.

'Yellamma is now leaving our realm. She will return next year. She is bidding us all farewell,' one of them explained. The wailing woman walked into the river and immersed herself fully. Once she did so, she emerged, still wailing. The others held her tightly. Suddenly, the wailing, the singing, the *veena* recital, all of it stopped abruptly. The women went about getting ready for their journey as if nothing had happened at all. We made our way back to the taxi after the ritualistic display of grief.

It was almost dusk by the time we reached Saundatti. From here on, the six-kilometre stretch to the Yellamma Gudda temple was entirely crammed up with street vendors. If there were no traders, buses and vans were parked indiscriminately on the road. An occasional policeman could be seen. We finally halted in front of a big gate with the temple's name written on it. We could hear cries of '*uda*' in the air, though not with the same fervour as in Uchangi.

Several women pushed us aside and ran ahead. We quickened our pace to follow them to an area where many showers had been fitted to a pipe. The women got under the showers quickly, some even removing their clothes as they showered without bothering if others could see them. Some policemen hung around the showers.

We asked the driver, 'Is this *ennakkonda* (a sacred pool)?'

'No. This water has been pumped from *ennakkonda*. The temple authorities add ghee to it and send it through the pipes. Lower castes believe that a shower under this water blesses them.'

Those who had finished bathing then ran to the temple, some wearing their wet clothes while others changed right outside the bathing area. There were some tents pitched on one side of the temple premises for travellers who had come for the festival. We could see people cooking and sleeping, just like in a normal house. Each tent had a horse carriage or a bullock cart attached to it. Humans and animals, all were tightly packed in that cramped space.

A little ahead, policemen slept on chairs in a shed. We woke them up and introduced ourselves. When they learnt we were from the press, they arranged some chairs for us too. We finally walked inside the temple at around 11.30 p.m. Women continued to run inside after bathing, but as soon as they crossed the temple's threshold, they immediately stopped running and started to walk slowly with folded hands. They would prostrate themselves on the ground after every three steps, repeating it over and over. Manoj told us this was the *dandaavathu* ritual that he had been trying to explain to us earlier.

I noticed a man who was making a young girl, who looked to be around eight, circumambulate the temple in *dandaavathu* just as an adult would. A wreath of neem leaves covered her waist, and she wore nothing else. The man accompanying her seemed to be her father. When they walked out of the temple, I followed them. It seemed a flood had hit the temple – there was so much water spilled outside from the pots of water that were poured over the heads of those who had completed the *dandaavathu* by their relatives. Drenched women conducted the ritual without caring for their clothes and their bodies. As the little girl emerged, someone handed her father a pot of water. As he poured it over her, the chill in the night air combined with the cold water made the child shiver. 'Maybe they will take her home and make her a devadasi. Or maybe they promised a *dandaavathu* when she fell sick,' Manoj noted.

We tried to talk to the father, but he refused to say anything and walked away, dragging the child with him. We went back inside. Now, a dance troupe had taken over the premises where the circumambulation had been going on. They were beating two huge drums, and the din was ear-splitting. People started crowding around them. We moved to a side. Two transgenders accompanying them slowly began to dance to the beat. More people began to crowd. Soon it seemed as if a wall of humans had surrounded the dancers. As the performance got more entertaining, people started putting 10-rupee notes into the dancers' pockets.

Within 10 minutes, their pockets spilled over with the notes. The show stopped and the crowd dispersed only when one of them fell down exhausted.

Outside, too, there was an air of festivity, with a performance by another dance troupe. Both men and women sang and danced here. One could make out they were experts at dancing in crowded areas. Though their expressions were seductive, they showed no skin. And although they did not object to us shooting a video at first, they asked us to stop after two songs.

When morning came, an even larger crowd began gathering at the temple. Roadside vendors had taken up every inch of space. We could see fewer old devadasis here than in Uchangi. Some vendors told us that since the officials had chopped off the matted tresses the previous year, many of them were afraid to return. I realized there was nothing more to learn about devadasis here, so we left the temple at 7 a.m.

I found out two months later that we had indeed missed out on a devadasi ritual on the full moon night of *Magha*, but in Davanagere. I learnt about it from Tommy, a bank officer whom I had met in Belgaum, who had read a report in *The Hindu* and called me. The news said that a 15-year-old girl had been made a devadasi in Kunjoor near Davanagere and the officials who had gone to investigate the complaint had been assaulted by the villagers in the belief that the goddess's anger had brought a drought to their village. The girl was reportedly living in one of the temples when the officials came to check, and then the villagers tied them up to stop them.

The incident racked up a controversy in Karnataka. The minister for social welfare and development visited the girl's house to do some damage control. He was told the girl was not a devadasi and that she was to be married off to her uncle as per the custom in those areas. The minister triumphantly repeated this to the press and left; the government needed to cover up any evidence that the ban on devadasis was not working. There were no further investigations. When the age of the girl became a controversy, the government announced the parents had promised to show them a birth certificate which proved she was over 18.

As far as I knew, she was the youngest devadasi in India. I decided I had to visit her to know how the younger generation felt about being sacrificed in the name of outlawed traditions. I set about looking for any contacts that could help me.

'The mother has threatened that both she and her daughter will commit suicide if one more journalist comes to their place. Don't visit right now,' the chairman of a Davanagere NGO cautioned the three of us when we first asked him. My colleagues Sivan Edamana and Pyarilal had decided to join me. And although we told him we were happy to just speak to the villagers, he began to prevaricate on the issue, giving some excuses we couldn't comprehend. So we decided to let him be and went to Kunjoor by ourselves.

From Davanagere, we took the Harapanahalli bus and got off at Nilkund. Kunjoor was about 10 kilometres away, and we sat on the roof of a packed-to-the-brim tempo traveller, which had both people and their livestock, such as goats and chickens, inside. There were vegetable farms all along the road, covering the landscape in green, except for a few spots where the land was uncultivated. When we arrived at Kunjoor, we saw that it was a village where the majority of homes were tiny two-room enclosures tied up with coconut leaves and the like. This settlement had no provision for washrooms or toilets. Poverty was stark everywhere.

A group of people had gathered near a temple. We introduced ourselves as being interested in learning more about agriculture there and asked them if they had any concerns. Most of them withdrew when they saw they were to be filmed. Some came ahead to say the drought was their biggest concern. Most of them were so dejected, they said if the rains didn't come they could do nothing but commit suicide.

We talked to several others as we walked around the countryside. Many were scared to speak on record. When a few came ahead, we asked them about the pujas that had been interrupted. This seemed to scare them, and they refused to talk any more. When we tried to hint about the devadasi story, all of them feigned ignorance.

The last bus to Davanagere would leave the village at 7 p.m. The villagers didn't sound like they were willing to say anything. There was nowhere we could stay in the village either, so we boarded the bus.

Five minutes after the bus left, it began to rain. 'See? The moment we asked about the rains, it has come. Will the villagers now tie us up thinking we have brought the rains?' Sivan asked sheepishly.

# 13

# The *Mujras* of Ujjain

UJJAIN IS A TREASURE HOUSE OF BOTH MYTHOLOGY AND history. Ujjain is as known for Vikramaditya, Kalidasa and Raja Bhoj as it is known for its profusion of temples. About 55 kilometres from Indore, Ujjain was the capital of the Avanti royal dynasty. It is one of the four holy cities that host the Maha Kumbh Mela, which it did in 2004.

I travelled alone to Ujjain in March 2015, and though I enquired in all the temples, I couldn't find any devadasis. I was then advised to check out the locality of Pinjarvadi, where devadasis were said to camp earlier. Pinjarvadi was not far from town, but even though I had clear directions, I lost my way a few times and had to ask the local shopkeepers, who would only smile and not say anything. Eventually, I arrived at a scrap iron store, and just after the store were a multitude of by-lanes. I randomly selected one of the lanes. A long, one-storeyed building with plenty of closed rooms stood on a side. In fact, each of these rooms seemed like an apartment in itself. Two windows were open; it was a small store with a middle-aged woman sitting inside.

'This is Pinjarvadi,' she confirmed when I asked her.

'I came here to see devadasis,' I told her.

'There are no devadasis now. You can see a *mujra* if you want.'

Since I wanted to ascertain whether the devadasis were indeed gone, I decided to go see the *mujra*. She pointed to a dark and dingy building in the adjacent lane. All the doors on the ground floor were shut too. '*Mujra* is performed upstairs,' she said, telling me one of the doors opened up into a staircase. I walked to the building and saw two open windows on the top floor. There was a small billboard in between, which read '*mujra*' alongside pictures of musical instruments.

In the hallway, I noticed a woman walking towards me. She wore a dirty and tattered salwar kameez and looked like she hadn't bathed in a while. She extended her hand asking for alms. But she moved on without waiting for a response. I could see some people doing something inside a room. When I went up, I saw they were putting away bananas. I chatted with them for a while about the banana business, and they were enthusiastic about the topic. I then asked them about devadasis, and they said there used to be devadasis here earlier but they didn't know where they had gone since. As we spoke, the begging woman walked past again, stretching out her palms to anyone who passed by.

When I asked the traders about *mujra*, they laughed.

'Is this legal here? Boards advertise it openly,' I asked.

'Yes, *mujra* can be conducted till 11 p.m.'

'What if I want to watch further into the night?' I pushed my luck.

'You can try. They may just agree,' one of them got the gist of what I was hinting at.

'Will the police catch me if I go now?' I wanted to be doubly sure.

'No. You need to fear the police only if you go after 11 p.m.'

I got up and walked to the door the traders had pointed out. I pushed it open. As if on cue, a woman's beautiful voice floated from somewhere, 'Who is it?'

When I said I had come to watch *mujra*, I was asked to come up. The stairs led up to a small hall and two more rooms. I was received by two beautiful young women between 20 and 25. The skinny one was called Shazia, and the other was Aditi. They said the *mujra* performance would cost me a hundred rupees per song. I agreed. Aditi said she would call the singers and made a few calls. The girls asked me to wait for five minutes and went inside. A little later, two men, one younger and the other older, walked up. They saluted me and took their seats across from me, pulling the tabla and the harmonium from a corner and tuning it. Once the tabla was tuned, the young man said something, and the two girls re-emerged. They had both touched up their faces and wore their shawls tightly wrapped around their bodies so as to display their curves. As soon as the old man said, 'One, two, three...' they began to dance to his song.

Though I could not follow the whole song, it went something like,

*I wish for you to be mine*
*Though I know it is not possible I wish for that.*
*We are all over the earth*
*We were born to bewitch man's heart.*

The same lines were repeated over and over. The music was nice, and the tabla was extremely invigorating. When I gave a hundred rupees after the first song, the girls asked if they could sing another. I agreed. After the song was over, I wanted to talk to them.

'Are you from here?' I asked them.

'No, we came here from somewhere else. We are not from here,' Aditi replied a little unwillingly.

'Where are you from?'

'Let that be. Shall we sing the next song?' She started getting impatient.

'Is there only music here?' I persisted.

'Yes. No scope for anything else, sir. The police will arrive without warning.'

'I have heard that devadasis used to be here long ago.' I tried my luck again.

'I don't know about that.' She made her disinterest clear.

I asked them to sing one more song. No sooner had I said it than the man on the tabla began playing a new rhythm. The girls immediately began to dance. As soon as they finished, they asked if they should repeat. They did not want to entertain any questions.

When I said that I would return in the evening with more money, Aditi laughed. 'Come before 11. Else you can't see the *mujra*.'

'I don't necessarily need to see the *mujra*. I will come with the money.' I left it at that, and she laughed in response.

Aditi brought some money from inside, which she gave to the men. They returned the instruments to their spots and left with me. The banana trader smiled at me as I walked out. The old man sat in the veranda of the shop next door. As I approached, he asked, 'Are you here to learn about devadasis?'

'Yes,' I replied. Across my visits, people were reluctant to part with any information, but here was this man who seemed like he was voluntarily coming forward.

'You have come to the right place but a few years too late.'

I watched him as if I understood nothing. He continued, 'Do you know of the 2004 Kumbh Mela here? The devadasis here were evicted that year. The police ousted them to clean up the place. Did that make a difference? Do you think this place has become better after that?' He took a deep breath in anger. 'Long ago, there were plenty of devadasis here in Ujjain. Initially, they became devadasis for the temple. Then, over time, all of them became prostitutes. Pinjarvadi became the street of devadasis who had turned into prostitutes. They knew how to sing and dance. They knew how to keep people happy. Some of them sang really well, and I played the harmonium for them too.' He told me this street was under the control of a woman named Suneeta. I remembered it was the same name the women in Kamathipura had told me about and got curious. The old man seemed eager to talk about her. 'Suneeta used to provide well for the girls – food, medicines when they were sick etc. She used to pay us artists well too. It was the decision to conduct the Kumbh Mela that destroyed everything. Uma Bharti's government feared that the *sanyasis* who came for the Mela would consort with these devadasis and be damned. That would be a big humiliation for Hinduism, they feared. Their solution was to kick out the devadasis. They used the police's brute force to evict them. The police went wild here that day. The women left as they were frightened by the thrashing and the rifles. But Suneeta could not leave this place. She stayed away for a while but came back after some time. By then, she had lost all that she had. She turned insane. You can still see Suneeta on this street – the same Suneeta who was once the queen of Ujjain.'

Was it the same beggar-woman whom I had seen earlier? Indeed it was, the old man confirmed. 'What was the result of evicting the devadasis to protect Hinduism? Instead, Muslims took over this place. They made houses and settled in some areas and opened shops in some places.' The old man then began to rant about his disappointments, but I was no longer listening to him. My thoughts centred on Suneeta and her decline. I felt like I had to see her one more time. I walked back to where I had seen her earlier. There she was, the erstwhile queen of Pinjarvadi, sitting next to a drain in an alley. She was not just sitting there. She in fact picked something from the drain, and after giving it a proper look over, popped it into her mouth.

Then she got up and walked ahead. I followed her. She walked into the hustle and bustle of the town, extending her hand to all those who passed by. Most did not notice her. At one point, someone placed a coin in her palm. She promptly handed it to a child who was passing by and stretched out her hands to others. That's when I noticed – despite begging for so long, she didn't have a single coin in her hands.

Oh! Empress of Ujjain, who, despite losing everything, including her own mind, still gave away so generously the meagre coins in her hand! Was this what this great kingdom of Vikramaditya and Raja Bhoj had in store for you – this filth from the drains?

Suneeta then walked back into the lane where she had been earlier. I could hear the tabla being played on the first floor. Soon enough, the song followed:

*I wish for you to be mine*
*Though I know it is not possible I wish for that.*
*We are all over the earth*
*We were born to bewitch man's heart.*

By then, the song had started making me feel uneasy. Aditi and Shazia continued their graceful dance, but all that I could see was Suneeta, the erstwhile queen of Ujjain, eating leftovers from the drain.

# 14

# Uchangi's Full Moons

THE SUPREME COURT PASSED AN ORDER ON 12 FEBRUARY 2016 that the Karnataka government was to ensure not a single girl was made a devadasi on *Maghapournami*, the full moon of *Magha*. Along with photographers Nikhil and Pyarilal, I visited Uchangi again that year to see how the court order was being implemented.

We reached the valley on the night before the full moon. Jogammas had begun climbing the Uchangi hill in great hurry, wielding the goddess's idol in their arms. There were a lot more policemen this time than the previous time I had visited – and several policewomen too, unlike last time. There was a big contingent of police at the *anehonde* on the way to the temple, listening to someone's instructions. I asked them for permission to click pictures, while Nikhil took out his camera, introducing ourselves as journalists from Kerala. The policeman pointed towards a person standing across from him – Harapanahalli Sub District Assistant Commissioner P.N. Lokesh.

Lokesh extended a handshake.

'Why so much police presence?' I asked.

'This is following the order from the Supreme Court. You said you are from Kerala, right? The Supreme Court interfered after an article appeared in one of the newspapers there,' he informed us. I listened to him without disclosing the fact that it was my article, titled 'What have we done to be made devadasis?' that appeared in the *Malayala Manorama* Sunday magazine on 2 February 2014. Lokesh was pleased when I asked him about the arrangements. He told us to note down everything. 'We will collect the details of all the girls being brought here today for *darshan*. We will go to their houses after a week to ensure they have not been made devadasis. Since we cannot stop anyone from coming to the temple, that's why we are collecting such details. We have appointed 10 teams for this purpose. Each team will have representatives from the departments of revenue, police, and women and child development. The government has also decided that one panchayat member and one member from the Devadasi Liberation Front will be a part of the team. One cameraman will also be present. We will have 24-hour announcements detailing the punishment for parents who try to turn their daughters into devadasis. Autorickshaws have been touring villages near the Yellamma temple announcing.'

Lokesh then got busy giving instructions to his subordinates while taking care to ensure he appeared in all the pictures. The women continued to walk up to the temple with trays of offerings, while the policemen diligently took down the details of the children accompanying them. We noticed two young women, not part of the police team, who were also noting down the details. One of them was the DYFI state vice president, Prajna Patil, who said she was determined that not a single girl would become a devadasi under her watch.

At the temple, the women were in a big hurry, running here and there. Everything else looked the same as before. I wondered what Renuka and her organization was doing. When I called her, she said she was at the venue and promised to see us soon. We waited for her among the crowd, and it seemed we were the only ones who were not in a hurry that day.

Renuka arrived in about 10–20 minutes, totally excited about the police surveillance. She said she would forever be indebted to Kerala for making this happen, since the article had first appeared in a Kerala newspaper. She distributed her organization's flyers to passers-by as we spoke.

When we returned to the temple at 7 a.m. the next day, there were even more women who were calling out '*uda, uda*' in peak fervour. We walked with them towards the temple – rather, we were being pushed along by the crowd. As we reached the temple, the speed of the crowd lessened.

But the cries of '*uda*' intensified. We could see women scattering off the moment they reached the entrance to smash the bananas at the back. Coloured powder flew in the air, while mashed bananas and broken bangles lay on the floor. It was not an atmosphere we could tolerate for more than a few minutes. But it was not possible for us to extract ourselves from the crowd.

It was then that I got a call from Uchangi Prasad, who had said we could meet him at the temple. Uchangi Prasad was a postgraduate student in journalism who had been assaulted by Sangh Parivar goons in December 2015 for writing a poetry collection titled *Hoddale Kicchu* (The Fire Within). He had been picked up from his college hostel by a group of people who took him to an isolated spot and broke his finger. In his complaint to the Davanagere police, Prasad said he was attacked because they did not want a lower-caste person like him writing poems. Based on the complaint, the Karnataka police had arranged a gunman for him. He had already been to Kerala twice to speak at programmes organized by the Progressive Literature Forum, but I couldn't meet him then. When I told him I was coming to Uchangi for the *Maghapournami*, he suggested we meet at the temple. We arrived near the *anehonde* and found Prasad announcing the legal repercussions of participating in the devadasi ritual on the mike. Prajna Patil, whom we saw the previous day, was also present. Prasad paused the announcements upon seeing us and came over to where we stood. He was dressed in pants, T-shirt and a sweater, probably to counter the cold of the night.

We walked down to the main road below the temple while talking. Prasad mainly spoke about the discrimination faced by lower castes in Karnataka. He was totally excited about his book, which had been released by K.S. Bhagwan, one of the most significant liberal thinkers in Karnataka. Six weeks later, he had been attacked.

'What was your inspiration to write poetry?' I asked him.

'Where else but from my mother's stories? My mother has told me plenty of stories about the discrimination she faced while growing up. My mother was a devadasi. And everyone in her generation believed they were destined to suffer miseries.'

I thought it would be good to meet her and asked Prasad if she would be coming to the temple.

'No, I have asked her not to take part in these celebrations. The people who come here are doomed to a life of tragedy in the name of faith. It is not acceptable that they come here to celebrate that event. Not everyone who comes here understands this. We cannot forbid everyone, but we can at least keep our own family away from this and send across a strong message. That is my purpose.'

'Your mother still believes in the goddess?'

'Of course. That will always be there. After all, the goddess did not make them devadasis. The wealthy people here did it in the name of the goddess, right?'

Prasad's mother was currently in the house of a relative, so if we wanted to see her, we would have to go there. We hired a car and set out to meet her. On the way, Prasad told us about himself, his mother and his poetry. He belonged to a caste called madiga. His mother's name was Yashodamma, and they currently lived in Santhebennur in Channagiri taluk. Prasad did not go to school as a child. His mother worked in the houses of wealthy landlords, and he used to accompany her and help her out. Though their wages were trivial, it was still a big relief for them. Then child labour was banned when Prasad was 12. Social workers rounded up several children like him. They were given lessons in music, dance and theatre for six months. After that, Prasad was admitted into the fifth grade at school. From then on, he focused all his passion into his studies. Yet, every day at bedtime, Yashoda would tell Prasad stories about her past. It was through the stories that he finally understood his mother's life.

Yashoda was made a devadasi at Uchangi, which was decided by her father and his relatives after her mother died. She had two younger sisters, and it was impossible for her poverty-stricken family to marry them all off. So, without telling her anything about the devadasi system, Yashoda was forced into a desolate life when she was merely 12. She learnt she was a devadasi only after the rituals were over. Till then, she had not been told anything about what was to happen with her. Several of those children who had been made devadasis like her had to beg for survival, while she had been able to make a living by daily labour because of the mercy of goddess Yellamma, she told Prasad. She considered it a blessing that she could work in the homes of higher-caste people. We reached the house where Prasad's mother was staying in about half an hour. But when she learnt we were from the press, Yashodamma hesitated to speak to us. It was after Prasad spoke to her for a long time that she agreed to come meet us. When we asked her about her past, she did not utter a word but only looked at her son, who answered all our questions. We asked her why she was so scared of us. But she was silent. Prasad lowered his voice and replied gravely, in a mixture of English and Kannada, 'Many of the devadasis are sex workers, which is why she is reticent to talk to you – since you have come to meet her in the capacity of a devadasi.'

We realized we would not get much information from her. Moreover, our presence seemed to agitate her. So we bid her farewell. Later, Prasad told us that his mother feared journalists. He clarified that he had used the term 'sex workers' in English so that his mother would not understand.

'What are the stories she has told you of the past?' I asked.

'The stories are all centred around our town – being served tea in a coconut shell, being served food outside the house... the usual stuff. Despite all of this, my mother believed she was lucky. Several like her begged for a living, so she thought she was especially lucky to get this job. My mother knew by heart the songs of the Uchangi temple. These experiences were what prompted me to write *Hoddale Kicchu*.' His eyes beamed with pride when he said his mother had received the first copy at the release.

Prasad, however, had not told his mother what the book was about. She was really frightened when he was attacked; she had learnt about it from her neighbours who had heard the news on TV. That was when she asked him what the book was about. She was convinced her son was in some serious trouble and chided him for writing on such a controversial topic. Prasad told us that the children of devadasis usually did not finish school and that he was really lucky to have completed his own education. He said there hadn't been much of a change in the way Dalits were treated in the interiors of Karnataka. 'In Kandakal, Davanagere, lower castes are not allowed inside barber shops. According to the barbers, if lower castes come in, upper-caste people will stop visiting their shop. So the Dalits have to go to Davanagere or another town for a haircut. The Anjaneya (Hanuman) temple in Kandakal still does not allow entry to Dalits. If a Dalit man marries a girl from a higher caste, his life ends there. He will have a rape case registered against him, and he will never again see the outside world. Dalits get lower pay at the workplace too. If others are paid 110 rupees, Dalits are paid 75. For women from lower castes, there are a host of other problems. My aunt's daughter was sexually assaulted by the landowner while working on his land. The most ironic part is that instead of taking offence, the woman asked me whether it wasn't part of the job for Dalits. She thought assault was a way of life for them.'

We reached Uchangi in the evening. The women had begun to walk down the hill, exhausted after the day's events. It wasn't no longer as crowded as the morning. We sat near the steps and continued talking about caste-based discrimination that was faced by several people from his community.

'One day, a ring went missing from the house where my mother worked. I was six or seven then. The child wearing the ring thought the ring was lost in the toilet. When he said this at home, they asked my mother to bring me. When I arrived, they asked me to put my hand inside the commode and look for the ring. I had no choice but to do it. Later, I asked my mother why I had to put my hand in the commode if there was another child of my age in that house. She said it was because we belonged to a backward caste. That was the day that I first thought about caste. Every person who comes from a lower caste will have a similar story to tell about the day caste began to scare them,' Prasad continued his saga. By the end, his voice got submerged in the '*uda*' cries.

Although the 2016 Supreme Court verdict had a remarkable impact in Karnataka, it would be naïve to assume the verdict alone could solve all issues. Although no new cases of devadasis were reported from the state that year, there could still be many who are willing to go against the law out of desperation and poverty. If anything, I'd like to draw satisfaction from the fact that my stories about the system were noticed by the court.

But if one were to keep one's eyes open, several uglier and more disturbing pictures are waiting to emerge. One example is the surge in child marriage in Karnataka after the ban on devadasis. People seem to have figured out that the easiest way to get rid of the burden of the girl child is to get her married off as early as possible. In several instances, the girl may be abandoned or forced to live as the 'wife' of several men. Thus, even if the paths are closed, the destination continues to stay out there.

What is implicit in these experiences is that more than the laws, we have to focus on the question of livelihoods to bring about any positive and sustainable change. There will always be several uncomfortable truths one encounters during such investigations. If there is anything these journeys have taught me, it is that a true journalist can never be complacent in the belief that a social evil has been uprooted. They will continue to sprout and flourish in one form or the other. It is only by eliminating poverty that one can arrive at a permanent solution.

Sonagachi and Kamathipura can be banned in a day. But in that case, the Charus who had to abandon their revolution in the name of hunger and the Diyas who were sold off by their own parents will have to sell their bodies in the streets. We can pretend not to see them and pledge with solemnity and dignity that 'all Indians are my brothers and sisters.' But they will continue to exist, even if we ignore them.

Female foeticide is banned in India. Yet, so many tiny lives are killed off without being given an opportunity to live. But having seen the ones who live endure suffering, one cannot help but feel the ones who died were luckier.

There is so much more that is unseen and untold. But the account of what was seen and observed thus far ends here.

# Acknowledgements

The book belongs to my dear friends as much as it belongs to me. There are many who have informed me whenever they find something related to the devadasi issue and have prompted me to probe further. Some of them were ever ready to accompany me on the journeys.

Pramod, who was with me on most of the trips, sometimes used to plan the trips himself and take me along. Often, he seemed more enthusiastic than me about bringing out the book. I am thankful to Rajagopal sir, editor of the *Telegraph*, and his wife Mini Elizabeth Ninan for providing me with a warm and comfortable stay while I was in Kolkata. I am not repeating the names of those who were with me and helped me in my journeys since they are mentioned in the book. The encouragement I got from T Ajeesh, my colleague at *Malayala Manorama* is invaluable. Also, I am thankful to my friend Sivan Kottiyur for his support. Special thanks also to Kanishka Gupta and Hachette India.